FRANÇOIS VILLON
AND HIS READER

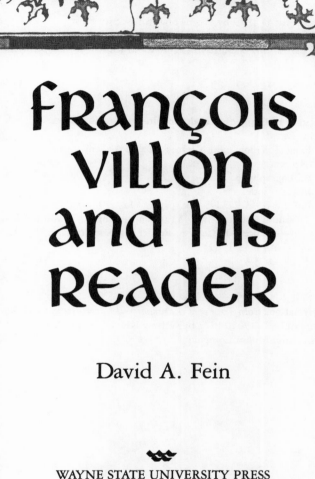

FRANÇOIS VILLON and his READER

David A. Fein

WAYNE STATE UNIVERSITY PRESS
DETROIT 1989

93   92   91   90   89   5   4   3   2   1

Library of Congress Cataloging-in-Publication Data
Fein, David A.
    François Villon and his reader / David A. Fein.
       p. cm.
    Bibliography: p.
    Includes index.
    ISBN 0-8143-2131-3 (alk. paper) : $27.50
    1. Villon, François, b. 1431. Grant testament. 2. Authors and
readers—France—History. 3. Reader-response criticism. I. Title.
PQ1590.A43F43 1989
841'.2—dc19   88-27649
                                                    CIP

Translations from *The Poems of François Villon,* translated by Galway Kinnell.
Copyright © 1965, 1977 by Galway Kinnell. Reprinted by permission of
Houghton Mifflin Company.

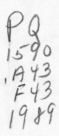

For My Mother

contents

preface

 he original objective of this study was to apply a reader-oriented approach to François Villon's *Testament*. At an early stage in my research, however, I realized that the study could take either of two directions. It could, as initially intended, focus on "the reader," that is, the general reader theoretically unaffiliated with any given historical period, or it could focus on the audience to whom the work was primarily directed. I opted for the second possibility, finding it more intriguing, challenging, and potentially productive than the first. The present study does not espouse any existing reader-response theory. Although various promising approaches have been developed under the general rubric of reader-response criticism—those of Iser, Jauss, Eco, Fish, Holland, and Bleich, to cite a few of the most prominent names—and although this study builds on the pioneering work of these critics, no established approach readily lends itself to the purposes of my analysis. The current methodologies, as the reader-response label implies, tend to concentrate on the effects of the text on the reader. The aspect of Villon's work that I find most interesting, however, is not how a reader—any randomly selected reader from any historical period—might read Villon but how Villon "reads" his audience, investing his poetry with meanings that only his intended readers are capable of understanding. In this sense, I am as interested in author response as I am in reader response.

The thesis of *François Villon and His Reader,* insofar as the study may be reduced to a single thesis, is that the *Testament* read by its original audience and the *Testament* read today are actually two very different poems. The first chapter attempts to identify Villon's "target audience," combining analysis of internal evidence with deductive reasoning. The next two chapters investigate the imagery and irony of the *Testament* as functions of reader participation. Chapter 4 focuses on various devices designed to engage the reader in the text. A passage of critical significance in defining the author's relationship with his intended reader, the "Belle leçon aux enfants perdus," receives separate treatment in Chapter 5. Chapter 6 considers a secondary audience addressed in Villon's poetry and contrasts the "anonymous reader" with the "privileged reader." Finally, for purposes of analogy and contrast, Chapter 7 briefly considers the role of the intended reader in the poetry of Villon's contemporary, Charles d'Orléans. In the conclusion I define as specifically as possible the differences separating the 1462 *Testament* from today's *Testament*.

Although recent years have seen a proliferation of reader-oriented studies, the vast majority of these pertain to works of modern literature. Very few attempts have yet been made to consider medieval literature from an audience-oriented perspective. Studies differing greatly in scope and critical methodology have been written on the *Inferno*, the *Libro de Buen Amor*, the *Roman de la Rose*, and the *Quinze Joyes de mariage*.[1] The present study represents the first known attempt to firmly establish the primary audience of the *Testament* and to investigate the role of this original audience in the work. The German scholar Gert Pinkernell has tentatively identified the audience of Villon's *Lais*, and, although he neither elaborates on the reasons for his conclusion nor explores the role of the audience in the *Lais*, he has at least broken a little new ground in Villon criticism.[2] I have chosen to basically limit my study to the *Testament*, but many general observations concerning Villon's second poetic will also apply to the *Lais*, which in many ways parallels its successor and which I believe was intended for the same audience.

In the first chapter I explain how the term "reader" is to be understood in the context of this study. Although I use several different terms for the sake of variety, my basic intent is to draw a distinction between the "intended reader" (alias "privileged reader," "first reader," "primary audience," "immediate audience") and the "anonymous reader," a category into which the "modern reader" is subsumed. I trust that my consistent use of the masculine pronoun in reference to the reader will not be mistaken for a sign of sexism. To any readers who may be offended by this practice, I would simply point out that the pronoun is accurately used when applied to Villon's intended readers and that in all other instances I am simply following the stylistic example of Louise Rosenblatt (a well-respected theorist of reader-oriented criticism) and others who prefer the simplicity of the generic "he" to "he/she." In referring to Villon's intended reader, I sometimes use the present tense. Again, this is a decision of style, intended to dramatize the reader's interaction with the text and to avoid repeated use of more awkward grammatical constructions. I will refrain from commenting on other stylistic idiosyncracies, except to ask my own reader's indulgence and patience for whatever incorrigible habits of expression may become apparent in the course of the study.

acknowledgments

all translated excerpts of Villon's poetry are taken from Galway Kinnell, *The Poems of François Villon* (Boston: Houghton Mifflin Co., 1977). I am grateful to Houghton Mifflin for the permission to include these excellent translations. All other translations are my own.

This monograph was largely written during a research leave in 1987, generously granted to me by the University of North Carolina at Greensboro. I am indebted to my colleague, Professor James C. Atkinson, for his advice and encouragement concerning my manuscript. I also wish to thank Professor Louise Rosenblatt for her encouragement during the early stages of this study. As in all my professional endeavors, I benefited greatly from the experienced advice of my father, Professor John M. Fein of Duke University, and from the maternal wisdom of my mother, Lucy. Finally, this work could not have been completed without the constant support of my wife, Rita, whose cheerfulness, sensibility, and sensitivity helped me to remain relatively sane throughout the writing of this book.

1
audience

ny reader-oriented study should begin with a clarification of the term "reader," a word all too loosely used in reader-response criticism. Many critics assume tacit agreement on the question of the reader's identity or else dismiss this identity as irrelevant, thereby considerably weakening the foundation on which all their hypotheses will ultimately rest. Stanley Fish defines his construct of the "informed reader" as someone who is a competent speaker of the language employed by the author, in full possession of the semantic knowledge required to understand the text, and who possesses literary competence.[1] The definition, while clearly specifying the qualities with which Fish wishes to endow his hypothetical reader, neglects the degree to which the reading of a given text will be influenced by the reader's historical relationship with the text, that is, the degree of distance (if any) separating him from the cultural values and social attitudes that underlie the literary work. In *Surprised by Sin: The Reader in Paradise Lost,* Fish fails to draw a rigorous distinction between the seventeenth-century and twentieth-century reader, implying that both would perceive the poem in the same basic manner, despite the appreciable cultural, social, and historical factors separating the two.[2] The construct of a universal reader, while possibly legitimate when applied to contemporary works of literature, poses serious risks when applied indiscriminately to literary works created during historical periods vastly different from our own, works we will always read as "foreigners," regardless of how much semantic knowledge we may possess. The further the

chronological distance separating us from the text, the greater
the risk of misreading, if we insist on using a "unilateral" approach in performing reader-response analysis.

In describing the reading process, Louise Rosenblatt acknowledges the influence of "the cultural, social and personal
context of the transaction."[3] From Rosenblatt's observation it follows that a medieval reader or listener could not be expected to
perceive a text in the same manner as a modern reader. To refer,
therefore, to "the reader" in Villon's *Testament* would be misleading, confusing, and perhaps meaningless, unless at the outset
I clarify the identity of the reader. The logical point of departure, then, for the present study is a consideration of Villon's intended reader, the audience to whom the poem was originally
directed.

The last statement implies, of course, certain assumptions
that may warrant a brief explanatory comment. First, I am as-
suming that Villon did not write only for himself. However obscure, hermetic, and inaccessible his poetry may appear to the
modern reader, Villon wrote with the intention of communicating. This does not mean that we, as twentieth-century readers,
will necessarily grasp the gist of a given passage; nevertheless,
the desire to communicate remains obvious. Much of Villon's
poetry may be fairly characterized as obscure but not opaque. The
hidden messages—the acrostics, examples of antiphrasis, veiled
allusions—would be pointless if not intended to be decoded by
an initiated audience, however restricted that audience might be.
Furthermore, as Wayne Booth points out, any work of literature
that has survived the test of time must incorporate at least a
minimal amount of rhetoric, thus proving that the work is more
than a private exercise in introspection:

> Regardless of how we conceive the core of any literary work, will it be
> entirely freed of a rhetorical dimension? On the contrary, at the very
> moment of its initial conception . . . a rhetorical aspect is contained
> within the conception: the subject is thought of as *something that can be
> made public,* [sic] something that can be made into a communicated
> work.[4]

Second, in my attempt to identify the immediate audience of the *Testament* I assume that the poet did in fact direct his writing toward a specific public. The reasons leading to this conclusion are basically the same as those used to justify the first assumption. The highly personal nature of the *Testament* presupposes certain knowledge on the part of the reader, without which the poem would lose considerable meaning. Unlike the modern author who essentially writes into a void, having no way to personally acquaint himself with his vast, diverse, and widely dispersed readership, the medieval author was able to direct his work to a small and relatively homogeneous public, many members of which might be personally acquainted with the author.

Despite its importance, Villon's immediate public has attracted surprisingly little critical attention.[5] Although it is clearly impossible to determine the precise identities of Villon's intended readers, a careful examination of internal evidence will lead to certain reasonably well-grounded conclusions concerning the general character of Villon's "target audience." The most revealing and numerous clues to the public of the *Testament* are the names cited in the poem. Names in the work fall into three categories: (1) those designating mythological, legendary, biblical, and historical figures; (2) those of well-known contemporary public figures; and (3) those of less prominent residents of Paris, many of whom were probably well acquainted with Villon. The third group obviously offers the most useful information.

The last category of names may in turn be broken down into four basic groups. The first group is comprised of "petits bourgeois," shopkeepers and guildsmen known to Villon but by no means prominent citizens of Paris: Jean Moreau, owner of a rotisserie; Jean de Provins, a baker; Robin Turgis, proprietor of the local tavern *Pomme de Pin;* Jacques Raguier, a royal cook who frequented Turgis's tavern; Catherine de Bruyères, owner of the hostel *Pet au Diable;* Colin Galerne, a barber-surgeon whose shop was on the same street as the *Pomme de Pin.* The second group consists of individuals with whom Villon was better acquainted: his mother, to whom he dedicates a ballade; Guillaume de Villon, the chaplain who adopted and raised the young François; Jean Cotart, the attorney who represented Villon in ecclesiastical court; Guy Tabarie, a participant in the Navarre robbery who eventually denounced Villon and the other accomplices; Colin de Cayeux, also involved in the Navarre affair and hanged in 1460 for crimes of larceny; Marion l'Idole and Jeanne de Bretagne, prostitutes; Catherine de Vausselles, probably a former girlfriend; Noël Jolis, an acquaintance who betrayed Villon in an unexplained incident involving Catherine de Vausselles. Members of the clergy constitute the third group: Frère Baude de la Mare of the Carmelite order; professor of theology Pierre Richier; ecclesiastical judge Pierre Lomer; bishop's attorney François de la Vacquerie. The fourth and largest group is comprised of individuals representing civil authority, members of the municipal police, and officials of the infamous prison and law court, the Châtelet— for example, Jean Raguier, Jean Valette, Pierre Basanier, Perrenet Marchant, Nicolas Rosnel.

If Villon intended that the vast stretches of the *Testament* in which he names his heirs and designates their gifts remain intelligible and accessible to his audience, then he must have expected the majority of names to be readily recognized. The initial step, therefore, in determining Villon's primary audience is to locate the intersection of the four groups of names outlined above. The only readers who could be in a position to recognize all the names, or at least the vast majority of names, would be the poet's friends. As fellow clerics and graduates of the *Faculté des Arts,* they would appreciate his satirical treatment of ecclesiastical officials, his parodies of scholastic reasoning, and especially (given the animosity between student and civil authority, a tradition proudly upheld by Parisian students to this day) his sardonic comments on the municipal police. As residents of the university quarter of Paris, they would be well acquainted with the various shops and taverns mentioned by Villon. Even a cursory glance at the list of local place names cited in the *Testament* reveals the prominence of taverns: *le Barillet, le Cheval Blanc, le Grand Godet, la Mule, la Pomme de Pin,* all surely familiar to the poet's drinking partners.

In addition to forming the locus of intelligibility for many names cited in the *Testament,* Villon's friends would be the only readers capable of comprehending the numerous autobiographical allusions scattered throughout the poem. The whole episode of Villon's imprisonment in Meung-sur-Loire, for instance, never receives the slightest explanatory comment, despite its obvious influence and recurring mention during the poem. The lack of circumstantial information, while perhaps perplexing to the modern reader, would seem perfectly natural to a reader well acquainted with the poet and fully apprised of the details surrounding his arrest and imprisonment during the summer of 1461. The Navarre affair, although never explicitly mentioned in the poem, clearly underlies Villon's hostility toward Guy Tabarie, the accomplice who "squealed." Again, the circumstances to which the poet implicitly alludes would be clear only to those familiar with his past. The incident involving Catherine de Vausselles and Noël Jolis, like the imprisonment of Meung-sur-Loire, remains today shrouded in mystery. Villon draws once more on the privileged knowledge of his reader to supply the omitted details.

Further corroboration of the nature of Villon's immediate audience is provided by two passages in which Villon directly addresses his readers. In the section of the poem popularly known as the "Belle leçon aux enfants perdus" Villon assumes the guise of a teacher instructing the *enfants perdus,* who are to be found "sur Marion l'Idole," the prostitute:

> Beaulx enfans, vous perdez la plus
> Belle roze de vo chappeau;
> Mes clercs pres prenans comme glus.[6]

> [Sweet children, you're throwing away
> The prettiest rose in your caps
> My clerks with fingers like glue.]

19

The teacher/pupil relationship is clearly a thinly disguised parallel to the poet/reader relationship. Granted, it is possible to naively construe the *enfants perdus* as dissolute individuals with whom the original readers of the poem are not meant to identify, but the equivocal use of *clercs* and the sense of irony and collusion that characterizes the passage argue against this interpretation.

The *leçon* is followed by the "Ballade de bonne doctrine à ceux de mauvaise vie," and then a final admonition:

> A vous parle, compains de galle,
> Mal des ames et bien du corps:
> Gardez vous tous de ce mau halle
> Qui noircist les gens quant sont mors. (1720–1723)

> [I mean you, comrades in revels
> Healthy in body but sick in soul
> Watch out all of you for that dry rot
> That turns men black when they're dead.]

The prepositional phrase that opens the stanza, "A vous parle," may be read in two different ways: (1) Villon is singling out a specific portion of his audience that he wishes to address at this point in the poem; or (2) Villon is alerting his readers to his awareness of their presence and, still playing the role of the pious pedagogue, emphatically and rhetorically urges his wayward pupils to heed his advice. Although the first explanation cannot be categorically refuted, it is more difficult to justify than the second. There is simply no compelling evidence that Villon has ever been addressing any other audience than the one to whom he is speaking at this moment. In fact, as I have tried to demonstrate, all evidence points to the *compains de galle* as the one audience to whom the *Testament* is consistently and logically directed.

Yet another source of information on Villon's intended audience for the *Testament* is the language itself. Hans R. Jauss has suggested that a literary text "be understood as creating a dialogue."[7] It follows, then, that the author's diction—his lexical range, tone, style, register, essentially every component of the author's voice—will be partially determined by the type of reader or listener engaging in the silent part of the dialogue. One has only to look at the shorter poems that Villon composed for a specific purpose and a designated public to perceive the extent to which he tailors his language to fit the audience. The "Requête à Monseigneur de Bourbon," asking the duke for a modest loan, the "Louange et requête à la cour de Parlement," requesting a three-day delay in his banishment from Paris, the "Dit de la naissance de Marie d'Orléans," composed in honor of Charles d'Orléans's daughter, are all written in a suitably elevated style; the requests or praises are couched in formalistic and even stilted language. The language of the *Testament,* by contrast, is heterogeneous, natural, lively, playful, and often gives the impression of complete spontaneity. It is the language of a man speaking in familiar terms to a familiar audience, a comfortable, even conversational discourse full of colloquial expressions, proverbs, slang, obscenities, innuendos. It is, in short, the language of intimacy. The unstated implication of this relaxed linguistic posture is: "You know me. You know what I've been through. You know what I'm really saying."

Despite the enormous popularity that the *Testament* quickly attained once in printed form, it is obvious from all available evidence that the poem was never intended for mass distribution. On the contrary, its subversive character, its many attacks on prominent municipal and ecclesiastical authorities, along with numerous manifestations of its authorship, would undoubtedly have brought the poet serious difficulties, had the manuscript ever fallen into the wrong hands. Given the politically sensitive nature of this seditious document, it is probable that the dissemination of the manuscript to its first readers was rather carefully controlled and even surreptitious. To be allowed access to the *Testament* would have required a certain trust, a trust reserved for those who could be relied upon not to betray the author of this potentially incriminating piece of writing. The intended audience of the *Testament,* then, by the very act of reading the poem was drawn into not only literary collusion but also political conspiracy. Once again, the preeminent condition for the poem's success, and in this case for the poet's security as well, was a close acquaintance between poet and audience.

Who were the *compains de galle,* these "comrades in revels"?[8] Pierre Champion describes the subclass to which Villon and his fellow clerics belonged:

> Les clercs ont formé à la fin du Moyen Age la classe par excellence des dévoyés et parfois des vagabonds. Les registres du Parlement et des officialités nous montrent que souvent leur conduite n'était pas différente des mauvais écoliers: comme eux, ils jouaient aux dés, ravissaient des jeunes filles, chantaient le soir, par les rues, des chansons moqueuses ou d'amour, portaient des bâtons et jouaient des farces qui tournaient parfois au tragique.[9]

> [The clerics at the end of the Middle Ages preeminently formed the class of "black sheep" and sometimes vagabonds. The registers of Parlement and of the courts show us that often their conduct was not different from that of naughty schoolboys: like them, they played at dice, forced themselves on young girls, sang at night, in the streets, mocking songs or songs of love, carried staffs, and played out farces that sometimes turned to tragedy.]

Insofar as limited knowledge of Villon's milieu permits, a very general but reasonably well-grounded profile of a typical fifteenth-century Parisian cleric may be outlined: The young man, readily identifiable by his tonsure, possessed at least a minimal university education; he was hardly well off, frequently unemployed, and forced to rely on his own resourcefulness to secure any income. Although the degree of his involvement, if any, in illicit activities would vary according to the individual, one may reasonably assume that he was well acquainted, if not through first-hand experience at least through the experience of more adventurous fellow clerics, with the darker side of Paris—its taverns, prisons, prostitutes, corrupt police, and a wide assortment of related criminal activities. The typical cleric, like Villon, occupied a marginal position in his society.[10]

In the introduction to his edition of Villon's poetry, Clément Marot draws attention to both the specificity of the bequests in the poetic wills and the corresponding knowledge of Villon's immediate milieu that they require in order to be properly understood:

> Quant à l'industrie des lays qu'il feit en ses testaments pour suffisament la cognoistre et entendre, il fauldroit avoir esté de son temps à Paris, et avoir cogneu les lieux, les choses et les hommes dont il parle: la mémoire desquelz tant plus se passera, tant moins se coignoistra icelle industrie de ses lays dictz.[11]

> [As for the ingenuity of the legacies that he made in his testaments, in order to understand and appreciate it, one would have to have lived in the Paris of his [Villon's] day and would have to have known the places, things, and men of whom he speaks; the more the memory of these things disappears, the less will be recognized the ingenuity of these legacies.]

Thus, even in 1533, only seventy years after the composition of the *Testament,* large portions of the poem had already been rendered inaccessible, if not totally incomprehensible, to a reader separated from Villon by barely two generations. Yet, a poem filled with allusions to people, places, and events that are practically unknown today has not only survived more than five centuries of changing literary taste but has also incontestably established itself in the canon of French literary classics. This fact would be completely baffling and unexplainable if not for the poem's dichotomous nature. The *Testament* is actually a melding of two distinct modes of poetic discourse. The will proper, including the lengthy prologue, constitutes the skeletal framework of the poem, providing a minimal structural unity and loosely tying together the sixteen ballades dispersed at irregular intervals throughout the work. However, in the ballades the *Testament* primarily achieves its greatest artistry, lyrical intensity, universality. Without them, the poem could never have attained the wide popularity and respect that it has enjoyed since its inception.

The present study focuses mainly on the will proper, rather than the inserted ballades. Although each ballade merits a separate reader-response analysis and these analyses would undoubtedly reveal a wide variety of techniques by which universal reader participation is elicited, such an ambitious critical endeavor would exceed the scope of this study's primary objective, namely to examine the relationship between the poet and his original audience. To comprehend the essential meaning of the "Ballade pour prier Notre Dame," for example, requires no personal knowledge of Villon or his mother. To understand the poet's vindictiveness toward Noël Jolis, on the other hand, requires a knowledge of the poet's past that we cannot possibly command.

It is a generally accepted axiom of reader-oriented criticism that a relationship between author and reader is established the moment any reader begins to read any text written in a comprehensible language. I do not, therefore, mean to suggest that the segments of the *Testament* on which I will concentrate evoke no response at all from a modern reader. Given the distance, however, that separates us from Villon's milieu, the modern reader, although aided in his struggle by the collective erudition produced by generations of Villon scholarship, finds himself involuntarily engaged in an adversarial relationship with the poet rather than enjoying the privileged collaborative relationship that bound Villon to his original audience. If the reading process, as Rosenblatt posits, is analogous to the performance of a musical score, then the modern reader has surely not been properly trained to "perform the text." [12] Owing to a lack of knowledge, the performance, reflecting the reader's limited understanding of the composition and his best attempt at interpretation, will at best poorly approximate the kind of performance anticipated by the "composer." It should be understood, therefore, that the term "reader," unless otherwise specified, will be used from this point to designate Villon's original reader, whose general identity I have attempted to establish.

The problematic nature of the reader's role in the *Testament* sets the work apart from the vast majority of medieval French texts, most of which were accessible to a far less restricted public. The *Chanson de Roland,* the *Roman de la Rose,* the works of Marie de France and Chrétien de Troyes, although all aimed at a relatively select audience, did not require a personal knowledge of the author's character or past in order to be fully understood and appreciated. All the essential elements of *Erec et Enide* could theoretically have been as easily apprehended by any well-educated speaker of the *champenois* dialect as by an intimate acquaintance of the author. A bourgeois contemporary of Villon, on the other hand, living in Paris but unfamiliar with the poet and his milieu, would lose the significance of many personal allusions of the *Testament,* finding himself thereby excluded from much interplay between author and reader. A contemporary reader living in the provinces (Orléans or Poitiers, for example) would understand even less of the poem. Both these hypothetical readers, perhaps surmising the existence but failing to grasp the meaning of the "inside jokes," would share the sense of estrangement experienced to some degree by Marot and all subsequent readers.

Nor can I satisfactorily explain the "closed" character of Villon's work as an inherent characteristic of medieval lyric poetry. Any student of early French verse will attest to the accessibility of Guillaume de Machaut, Christine de Pisan, Eustache Deschamps, and Charles d'Orléans, compared to François Villon. However personal the poetry of these writers may be, it generally allows entry to those who show patience and perseverance, and difficulties generally arise from unfamiliar vocabulary and syntactical constructions more than from deliberate concealment of the poet's thought. Medieval lyric poetry, from its troubadour origins through the fifteenth century, tends to merge affective content with abstract expression. Charles d'Orléans, writing during his exile in England, protests the inadequacy of poetry as the only means of communicating with his wife:

> Se vouloye raconter plainnement
> En cest escript mon ennuieux martire,

Trop long seroit; pour ce certainnement
J'aymasse mieulx de bouche le vous dire. [13]

[If I wished to fully recount
My painful martyrdom in this writing
It would be too long; certainly for this reason
I would prefer to tell you by word of mouth.]

Although the context and message of the poem are highly personal, the poet's thought remains translucent, if not transparent, to the "unprivileged reader" whose ignorance of the specific circumstances surrounding the ballade does not deny him entry into the poem.

To some who are familiar with Villon's work, the observation that the *Testament* is directed primarily to the poet's circle of close acquaintances may appear so evident that any justification will be considered superfluous. I have chosen, however, to present the observation as a hypothesis, an a posteriori conclusion, rather than as a self-evident premise, for several reasons. First, there exists to date no thorough investigation into the nature of Villon's primary audience. A methodical examination of internal evidence from which the identity of this audience may be deduced, even if amounting to no more than a pro forma exercise, yields a certain amount of information about Villon's relationship with his intended public, information vital to the present study. Second, more than any other medieval French writer, Villon has repeatedly proven his ability to divide and stir controversy among literary critics. Thus, to take any assumption for granted presupposes a unanimity of critical opinion that is becoming increasingly rare among those who study Villon's poetry. Finally, since the bulk of the present study rests on the premise that the *Testament* is directed to a specific audience very different from the twentieth-century public that has inherited the work, I would be remiss if I did not attempt to validate this premise, and to draw as sharply as possible the distinction between the two readerships. To naively and irresponsibly ground the entire study on nothing firmer than an appeal to the charity of my own intended audience would place the whole critical enterprise in danger of almost certain collapse. Having, I hope, established a reasonably secure basis for my investigation, I will now examine in greater detail the interplay between Villon and his reader.

2

IMAGERY

One aspect of Villon's work that distinguishes it most from the mainstream of medieval lyric poetry is its pictorial character. While other poets rely heavily on abstract language, favoring an intellectualized representation of emotional conflicts, Villon, although proving adept in the use of abstract language, generally gravitates toward more graphic imagery. Guillaume de Machaut describes, in typical courtly fashion, the debilitating effects of love upon its victim:

> Hélas! dolens, que porray devenir?
> Quant si pleins sui d'amoreuse dolour
> Que je ne puis vivre ne mourir.[1]
>
> [Alas! sorrowful, what will I become?
> When I am so full of loving sorrow
> That I can neither live nor die.]

Villon, by contrast, employs a concrete and vivid image, transforming a standard courtly conceit, the arrow of love, into a painfully corporal experience:

> L'espoignoit d'Amours l'esguillon;
> Plus agu que le ranguillon
> D'un baudrier lui faisoit sentir. (2015–2017)
>
> [The spur of love pricked into him
> Sharper than a buckle-tongue
> Of a baldric he could feel it.]

Each of the hundreds of images contained in the *Testament* presupposes that the poet and the reader share a common "image-field," a term Hans R. Jauss defines as, "the associations called forth by certain words which have an adequate connotative potential. They evoke in the reader a self-contained sphere of ideas which are often recognized when just one *single* [*sic*] element of a system is presented (for example, *carillon* for the entire image-field *horloge*)."[2] This chapter, then, will focus on the type of image in the *Testament* that requires a privileged knowledge on the part of the reader in order to be fully and properly actualized.

The whole concept of imagery, in the broadest sense of the word—mental images, as produced by memory, imagination, or a combination of both—has recently become a focal point of psychological research, generating much interest and controversy in various scientific communities. Unfortunately, little is now known about image-forming processes in the human mind; thus, psychologists have little reliable information to pass on to their colleagues in literary criticism.[3] Several generally accepted theories, however, provide some guidance for the purposes of the present chapter. Ian Begg in his illuminating essay, "Language and Imagery," points out that linguistic communication depends to some extent on a successful interaction between language and images:

> The referential meaning of a message is the result of any knowledge made available by connections between the verbal and imaginal systems and further connections within the two systems. In actual use, comprehension is much more than an intralinguistic process. Comprehension occurs when enough referential information is made available to perform any discriminations required by the comprehender.[4]

Begg also draws a useful distinction between two types of meaning conveyed by a specific act of verbal communication. "Representational meaning" relates to the "nonarbitrary" content of the message: for example, the word "chair" evokes a mental picture of some sort of chair. But "associative meaning" results from the activation of a series of related words or images.[5]

These two generalizations, admittedly a drastic simplification of an immensely complex psycholinguistic phenomenon, yield several relevant implications when applied to the study of poetry and to Villon's verse in particular. First, it becomes immediately apparent that a purely philological approach to Villon's poetry, useful and necessary though it may be, remains generally confined to a single dimension of the text, that is, its representational meaning. Villon's work—any good poetry, in fact—contains a wealth of associative meaning evoked by the actual text. The exploration, then, of the associative dimension of this poetry constitutes the major challenge confronting Villon criticism today. To the extent that the *Testament* remains accessible to the modern reader, fragments of the poem may be illumined with remarkable clarity, as David Kuhn and others have amply demonstrated. To the extent, however, that the poem relies on connections between "the verbal and imaginal systems," connections existing for the poet and his immediate audience but not for the modern reader, the work inevitably resists attempts at elucidation.

Even though we cannot hope to recover the original "reading" of numerous passages of the *Testament,* we may at least examine the various ways in which Villon relies on reader participation. As far as imagery is concerned, two distinct patterns may be identified. First, some images lie fully within the grasp of any reader. Although a reader may fail to seize the visual essence of the image—given difficulties of language, lack of literary sophistication, undeveloped critical abilities, or many other reasons—the pictorial content of the verse remains, nonetheless, theoretically apprehensible. This type of image is exemplified by the passage quoted above, in which Villon juxtaposes love's arrow with the tongue of a belt buckle. The essence of the image is clear to any reader capable of visualizing any type of belt buckle. Exactly what Villon means by the image, of course, is subject to discussion. Kuhn interprets the passage as a reference to sexual arousal in extremis.[6] I have suggested elsewhere that the image connotes phallic penetration and may therefore be understood as a brutal sexual assault on the *povre Villon*.[7] The important point is that Villon constructs the image in such a way that it may be readily comprehended by both privileged and unprivileged reader. This type of image, which for the purposes of this chapter I will label an "open image," is especially prevalent in the ballades, the portion of the *Testament* most accessible to the modern reader. By contrast, the "closed image," prevalent in the will proper, is oriented toward the intended reader. The shape and clarity of this image depend largely on the reader's ability to connect the text to the appropriate imaginal system (to use Begg's term), the appropriate image-field (to use Jauss's term).

In the lengthy prologue of the *Testament* Villon describes himself as:

> Povre de sens et de savoir,
> Triste, failly, plus noir que meure. (178–179)

> [Poor in sense and in knowledge
> Sad, sick, blacker than a mulberry.]

The word *noir* also appears in an earlier self-description in the closing stanza of the *Lais:* (316) Sec et noir comme escouvillon [Dry and black like a furnace mop]. Although Villon makes frequent use of the first person in his two poetic wills, he applies relatively few adjectives to himself. Thus, the qualifier *noir* cannot have been randomly chosen and clearly constitutes a self-portrait, a self-caricature, or something between the two. Beyond this general and very limited observation, the modern reader can only speculate on possible meanings of the association. Louis Thuasne merely states that the phrase is a proverb and cites several examples from other medieval French sources.[8] Jean Rychner, relying mainly on the immediate context of the phrase, interprets "plus noir que meure" as "affreusement sombre."[9] Evelyn Vitz suggests that Villon may be presenting a "melancholic" temperment, connected in medieval medical science to black bile and a darkened complexion.[10] Kuhn focuses on the word *escouvil-*

lon in the verse from the *Lais* quoted above and discovers what he believes to be the hidden sexual implications of the analogy.[11] From this cursory review of selected commentaries, it should be evident that the images in question, while stimulating considerable interest among modern readers, remain something of a mystery. Whatever uncertainty we may harbor concerning the interpretation of the love's arrow/buckle-tongue image, we can at least understand that it represents yet another victimization by love, a victimization repeatedly illustrated throughout the *Testament*. To this extent, we may reasonably claim to understand the image.

The comprehension of the two images cited above, however, presupposes a personal knowledge of the poet. Villon, after all, had reasons for using the adjective *noir* in reference to himself and expected those reasons to be apparent to his reader. Even without understanding the thrust of the image, a perceptive modern reader will nonetheless perceive that *noir* is a pivotal word and that the image loses its force unless the word is properly grasped. Aware of the poet's physical appearance, able to distinguish whether or not the color corresponded in any way to the poet's actual state of health, knowing Villon's character and temperament, familiar with the connotations of the proverb "plus noir que meure" and with the function, appearance, and associations normally attached to the *escouvillon* [stove broom], the intended reader would be able to "perform any discriminations required by the comprehender" (Begg's phrase). In light of Villon's penchant for equivocal language, one may justifiably assume that the image plays on multiple readings. The intended reader serves as the ideal locus for these readings.

Another briefly sketched self-portrait occurs in the mock requiem prayer quoted toward the end of the *Testament:*

> Il fut rez, chief, barbe, sourcil,
> Comme ung navet c'on ret ou pelle. (1896–1897)

> [They shaved him, head, beard and eyebrows
> Like some turnip you scrape or peel.]

Again, the modern reader is cofronted by a closed image. The passage has elicited a variety of speculative explanations. Critics have suggested, for example, that the verses refer to a punishment administered by an ecclesiastical court, a shaven head in Villon's day representing, among other things, the loss of clerical status. If this is the case, it may well be that the punishment was ordered by Thibaut d'Aussigny while Villon was held in the bishop's prison during the summer of 1461. They have also pointed out that individuals thought to be mad or accused of witchcraft were required by medieval custom to have their head shaved.[12] The condition of baldness and loss of facial hair may also have been linked to disease, and Thuasne points out that medieval belief interpreted the condition as resulting from an abuse of physical gratification.[13] The passage need not, of course, be taken literally and may simply express in figurative language the state of absolute poverty that Villon claims and laments frequently during the course of the poem. In summary, the baldness of head and face may correspond, either accurately or exaggeratedly, to Villon's actual appearance, may refer to a previous incident, may imply a condition resulting from a punishment or from natural causes, may represent a figural expression of poverty, or may constitute a simultaneous reference to the poet's present physical condition and a commentary on his state of poverty. One must also recognize that the list of possible explanations of the passage, although representing the collective erudition and ingenuity of several highly competent scholars, is not necessarily exhaustive, and the intended meaning of the passage may well have eluded all those who have attempted to shed some light on these verses. To put it bluntly, we simply do not know what Villon is talking about. The image, like the other two self-descriptions quoted above, presupposes a knowledge on the part of the reader that will allow him to decode the meaning of the passage.

Not only does a personal knowledge of the poet allow the reader to grasp the meaning of a closed image, it must inevitably influence the mental formation of the image itself. A modern reader, however familiar with Middle French, with Villon's work, and with the extensive body of scholarship surrounding this poetry, cannot, obviously, visualize the poet's actual face when reading this passage. The image, to the extent that any image is formed here, may be that of a shaved head and a hairless face, a picture that will vary in detail, or lack thereof, from one reader to another. One reader, for example, may visualize a practically featureless face, similar to a comic-strip caricature; another may mentally adapt his memory of the famous engraving from Pierre Levet's 1489 edition of Villon's poetry; still another might see in his mind's eye a strikingly graphic representation, based perhaps on a cinemagraphic image or the memory of an actual acquaintance with whom, for some reason, he associates François Villon. In *5 Readers Reading* Norman Holland has admirably demonstrated the extent to which a reader's total personality and formation are brought to bear on the act of reading.[14] Despite idiosyncratic discrepancies, modern readers share a common element when confronting any closed image—all are forced to rely solely upon their imagination in order to generate an image from the text. The intended reader, to the contrary, would be incapable of completely dissociating the textually created image from his memory of the poet's actual features. Regardless of the degree to which Villon's real appearance corroborates or belies the veracity of the shaven head and face, his physical appearance, whether visualized in actual or altered form, represents an integral part of the imaging process. Indeed, the image derives its basic thrust from the reader's ability to make some sort of associative connection between the text and a mental picture of a known face.[15]

Other images, while not directly related to the reader's relationship to the poet, draw on a common source of knowledge uniting Villon with his reader. The legacy left to Jacques Raguier, for instance, relies heavily on the reader's familiarity with not only the legatee but also his character, appearance, and habits:

> Item, je donne a maistre Jacques
> Raguier le *Grant Godet* de Greve,

Pourveu qu'il paiera quatre placques,
Deust il vendre, quoy qu'il lui griesve,
Ce dont on coeuvre mol et greve,
Aler nues jambes en chappin,
Se sans moy boyt, assiet ne lieve
Au trou de la *Pomme de Pin*. (1038–1045)

[*Item* I give to master Jacques
Raguier "The Big Wine Cup" at Grève
Provided he pay four *plaques*
Even if it means he must sell
To his sorrow what covers calf and shin
And go bare-legged in little shoes
If he drinks without me sitting or standing
At our watering-spot "The Pine Cone."]

From the three allusions to Raguier found in Villon's work, certain general conclusions may be reached concerning the reputation of this individual. In the *Lais* Villon bequeathes to him, among other gifts, the *Abreuvoir Popin,* a watering place for horses on the banks of the Seine. He also leaves:

Paiches, poires—sucré, figuier—,
Tous jours le choiz d'un bon loppin,
Le trou de la *Pomme de Pin*. (155–157)

[Together with peaches, pears from the big fig tree
And always his choice of something sweet
At the tavern "The Pine Cone."]

Taken in conjunction with the references to eating and drinking found in the passage from the *Testament,* these verses suggest an individual reputed for his fondness of food and drink.[16] Along with Jacques James and Philippe Bruneau, Raguier is named one of three alternate executors of Villon's will whom he describes as:

Troys hommes de bien et d'onneur,
Desirans de sauver leurs ames
Et doubtans Dieu nostre seigneur. (1945–1947)

36

[Three men of wealth and honor
Who desire their souls' salvation
And fear God.]

Dufournet, extrapolating from this obvious example of antiphrasis, characterizes the three as "canailles sans foi ni honneur,
méchants et débauchés, mécréants et blasphémateurs, prompts à
s'approprier le bien d'autrui" [17] ["rabble without faith or honor,
wicked and debauched, unbelieving and blaspheming, quick to
seize other people's property"]. Raguier, who figures rather
prominently among Villon's "heirs," clearly makes an ideal target
of ridicule. The success of Villon's trenchant attack, as will become apparent, depends on considerable participation from his
reader.

The first two verses incorporate a conflation of two images—Jacques Raguier and the tavern of the *Grand Godet:*

Item, je donne a maistre Jacques
Raguier le *Grant Godet* de Greve. (1038–1039)

To the reader acquainted with the individual and the site in question, each name carries a cluster of related connotations. The
actualization of the composite image draws on the reader's visual
memory and the various associations connected with these names.
The network of associative connotations—all evoked by the name
of the individual, the name of the site, and especially the connection between the two—can only be activated by a reader who has
"experienced" both Jacques Raguier and the *Grand Godet.* Although the semantic meaning of the text is readily discernible,
its imaginal richness is predicated on a "privileged reading."

Having made the initial bequest, Villon stipulates that unless Jacques complies with certain conditions, he will be required
to pay four *placques.* The word, designating both copper coins
and scabs, prepares the humiliating scene sketched by the next
three verses, in which the unfortunate Raguier, forced to walk
bare-legged through the streets of Paris, must publicly display

the unsightly skin disease that covers his legs. Adding absurdity to indecency, Villon parades his victim *en chappin,* in dainty slippers. The image, although its intent may be immediately transparent to the modern reader, is charged with a humor that can only be appreciated by the intended reader. To imagine an unknown individual subjected to an act of degradation inspired by unexplained personal malice does not create an inherently comical situation. To fulfill the humorous potential of the scene—a potential we can clearly sense, even if incapable of participating in its full realization—the reader must intimately appreciate the absurdity of the scene. In other words, he must be able to visualize the victim, knowing both his personality and his appearance, subjected to the indignity he so richly deserves. Just as there are open and closed images in Villon's poetry, there is also open and closed humor.

The last two verses of the stanza have proven especially resistant to exegetical attempts:

> Se sans moy boyt, assiet ne lieve
> Au trou de la *Pomme de Pin.* (1044–1045)

If the phrase "Se sans moy boyt" signals some sort of authorial intent, as it surely must, then it may be assumed that Villon's imagined absence somehow plays against his imagined presence in the company of Jacques Raguier. The credibility of the implied scene—François Villon and Jacques Raguier drinking together at the *Pomme de Pin*—the significance of suggesting two positions in which Raguier might drink, the possibly equivocal use of *trou,* and the reasons for citing the *Pomme de Pin,* all hinge on the reader's knowledge of the two individuals in question and especially their relationship to each other. Deprived of such specific knowledge, a reader can merely sense the ironic tenor of the verses.

Perhaps the most striking imagery based on reader participation occurs in Villon's description of the *Grosse Margot.* Although the identity of this character has never been conclusively

38

established, Jean Rychner presents persuasive arguments in favor of accepting the reality of Margot's existence.[18] To Rychner's reasons I may add that the obvious irony with which Villon describes his "lady" would be uncharacteristically weak and ineffective, were it not based on an actual person. The repeated references to Margot's grace, beauty, and refinement are clearly calculated to play against the image of her actual physical appearance:

> Item, a la Grosse Margot
> Tres doulce face et pourtraicture (1583–1584)

> [*Item* to Fat Margot
> Sweet-natured full-face or profile]

> Je l'ayme de propre nature,
> Et elle moy, la doulce sade (1587–1588)

> [I love her for her own self
> And she me the sweet little one]

> Se j'ayme et sers la belle de bon het (1591)

> [Because I love and gladly serve this woman]

> Elle a en soy des biens affin soubzhet. (1593)

> [She has something for the nicest taste.]

Two images are consistently and forcefully juxtaposed in these verses. The conventional portrait of idealized feminine beauty and charm is sharply undercut by the actual image of the *Grosse Margot,* reflecting her true appearance and character. The tension between the two conflicting representations derives from the opposition of the "textual image," the courtly fiction, and the "latent image" the reader brings to the passage. The reader's participation, his deflation of the courtly illusion by juxtaposing the *belle* and the *Grosse Margot,* activates the irony of the passage.

The ballade culminates in a famous scene that portrays, in

unforgettably graphic fashion, the domination of the *povre Villon* by his "lady":

> Et au resveil, quant le ventre lui bruyt,
> Monte sur moy, que ne gaste son fruyt,
> Soubz elle geins, plus qu'un aiz me fait plat. (1616–1618)

> [And when we wake and her belly calls
> She gets on top so as not to spoil her fruit
> I groan underneath pressed flatter than a plank.]

The image, as vivid as any in the *Testament,* attains its full force and humor by depicting a specific man and a specific woman physically positioned to each other in a very specific manner. Although the scene may be partially reconstructed by the imagination, it can only be authentically created, that is, endowed with a reality that corresponds in substantial degree to the immediately known world, in the mind of a reader who can draw on memory as well as on imagination.

From the preceding discussion some may simply conclude that a modern reader cannot hope to recapture the sharpness of imagery that would have been perceptible to the intended reader. This conclusion vastly underestimates the gap separating the two modes of perception. The issue here is not merely a difference in degree but a difference in kind. To grasp the idea, one must first distinguish between the *text* and the *poem.* Rosenblatt succinctly defines the essence of each:

> "Text" designates a set or series of signs interpretable as linguistic symbols. . . . Thus in a reading situation "the text" may be thought of as the printed signs in their capacity to serve as symbols.
>
> "Poem" presupposes a reader actively involved with a text and refers to what he makes of his responses to the particular set of verbal symbols. . . .
>
> The poem, then, must be thought of as an event in time. . . . It happens during a coming together, a compenetration of a reader and a text.[19]

Building on this distinction, one may accurately assert that the *Testament* read by Villon's intended audience and the *Testament* read today, although basically identical as texts, constitute in fact two different poems. At some points the readings closely converge, and at such points, as I will later discuss, the distinction between the intended and the modern reader will no longer serve any useful function. In the case of imagery, however, the distinction is critical.

One way to understand the two different perceptions of Villon's imagery is to conceive of his poetry as a vast painting, a painting that has unfortunately been poorly preserved and has consequently fallen into a state of advanced decomposition. Although some portions of the painting are still fairly vivid, most portions of the work have lost all definition and coloration, having been reduced to barely perceptible outlines and rare, extremely faint traces of pigment. So vague are the outlines, so sparse the remaining details, that not even the most skilled artisan could possibly restore the original design.

The *Testament*, then, as experienced by the modern reader is a poem that yields many vague, blurred images. One may even go a step further, arguing that many of the poem's original images have disappeared completely, leaving us long stretches of imageless poetry. This conception of the poem, foreign though it may appear to readers accustomed to hearing Villon's poetry repeatedly described as "vivid," "colorful," and "graphic," may be justified if the word "image" is redefined. If the term is taken to designate a mental image connected by memory to an actual person, place, object, or event, then the poem is indeed filled with images but ones that have long since become invisible.

Filled with images of familiar individuals, sites, shared experiences, the *Testament* draws the intended reader into a poetic world in which he finds constant reflections of his own world. The poetic reality that he discovers, of course, does not accurately mirror the reality from which the images are taken. Prostitutes become refined and cultivated ladies, wealthy merchants become destitute orphans, sadistic jailers become men of conscience and compassion. Yet, however gross the distortions, the faces remain familiar to those intended to recognize them. The imagery of the *Testament,* fully realizable only in the minds of the author and the intended reader, binds the two together, at the same time excluding all who do not share the immediate chronological, geographical, and social context of the poem.

3

IRONY

Perhaps the aspect of the *Testament* that contributes most to the work's complex and problematic character is the use of irony. If an ironical tone were consistently applied with even force throughout the work, there would be little difficulty in reading the authorial intent behind any given passage. The poem, however, encompasses a wide spectrum of ironic hues, ranging from heavy-handed parody and open mockery to the subtlest suggestion of possible ambiguity. A significant number of passages even appear altogether free of ironic overtones. The obvious result of Villon's adept manipulation of irony is that any reader, whether living in the fifteenth or the twentieth century, is forced to make frequent interpretive judgments regarding the author's intent.

Such readerly interpretations may often be reached with relative ease and confidence. When Villon speaks of the beauty and charm of the *Grosse Margot,* the honesty of the Parisian police, and the prayer he will offer for Thibaut d'Aussigny, the ironic overtones are unmistakable. But when he speaks about himself, one usually finds that the true intent cannot be so easily grasped. Does the confession of sin reflect a genuine state of contrition, or is it colored, however discreetly, by a subtle touch of irony? [1]

> Je suis pecheur je le sçay bien,
> Pourtant ne veult pas Dieu ma mort,
> Mais convertisse et vive en bien,
> Et tout autre que pechié mort. (105–108)

[I am a sinner I know it well
And yet God doesn't want me to die
But to repent and live right
And so with all others bitten by sin.]

Any reader, when confronted by such seemingly disarming candor, must determine whether to accept the confession at face value, take it instead as a travesty, or situate the author's intention somewhere between the two extremes. Without the benefit of reliable guidance, one must make certain assumptions about not only the passage but also the nature of the entire poem and the character of the author himself. The reader thus ultimately finds himself making a series of educated and less educated guesses.[2] Evelyn Vitz summarizes the predicament of the modern reader: "It might be said that some of Villon's descriptions and autobiographical remarks are serious, and clearly true; others jokes, and clearly not. But in Villon's poetry do we really always know when Villon is joking and when he is serious? I think not. The tone in this poetry is too complicated to allow for any stable and reassuring dividing line."[3]

One way in which current criticism has reacted to this element of ambiguity is by attempting to distinguish between the poet, the historical François Villon, and the persona, the *je* of Villon's poetry. The narrative voice, we are told, can never be fully trusted. Everything the narrator says should be, as William Calin puts it, "taken with a grain of salt."[4] The distinction between poet and persona appears to render irrelevant any questions regarding the relationship between the poetic "I" and the historical poet. Norris Lacy attempts to explain the realism of Villon's *je* as an illusion skillfully created by the poet: "The test of a convincing persona is that it *could* [sic] be real, even though, as a matter of principle it never is. It is the result of techniques that define and develop it with a realism sufficiently pervasive to particularize it, to endow it with a specific literary existence, and to create as a result the impression of its identity with an implied author."[5] Although Booth's differentiation between the author

44

and the narrator provides a useful distinction, especially when applied to the interpretation of contemporary fiction, the concept sheds little if any light on the author/reader relationship in the *Testament*. First, if the poetic "I" of the poem is taken as a mask, then it is an often transparent mask. When the narrator of the poem recalls his suffering in the prison of Meung-sur-Loire, expresses his bitterness toward Thibaut d'Aussigny, his gratitude to Louis XI, and his resentment for Guy Tabarie, and speaks of his relationships to his mother and Guillaume de Villon, there is no valid reason to assume that we are hearing the voice of a fictitious character rather than François Villon himself. The assumption of authenticity does not, of course, imply that every assertion of the narrator must be naively accepted as true, any more than the physical presence of the actual poet would necessarily validate the veracity of every spoken statement. Also, while an authentic voice may be perceived at scattered intervals, other disguised voices may also be detected—that of the dying old man, for example. Still, Calin's observation that every statement found in Villon's poetry must be taken with a grain of salt represents an overreaction to the irony of Villon's work. To read irony and concealed meaning into every passage of the *Testament* would not only do injustice to the tonal complexity of the poem, reducing the rich diversity of narrative registers to a monotonously repetitive pattern, but would also result in a poor reading if not a misreading of the entire poem.

Second, the concept of persona in no way contributes to resolving the modern reader's dilemma, that is, how to distinguish authenticity from irony in those important passages of the poem where Villon speaks of himself—his past, his sufferings and failures, his present condition, his fears and aspirations. To posit the existence of a literary construct that artfully creates the illusion of reality fails to help us discern connections between the *je* of the poem and the historical Villon, connections whose existence, nonetheless, is unmistakable.

Finally, the most serious problem with the concept of persona, whatever valid applications it may have for the modern reader struggling to make sense of a complex and perplexing poem, is that it proves misleading when applied to the relationship between Villon and his intended reader. This relationship, as I hope to demonstrate by the end of the present study, is based on a largely unmediated encounter between two personally acquainted individuals and functions effectively to the extent that it exploits the mutual understandings inherent in this relationship. Thus, the irony of the *Testament* is based mainly on the poet's expectation that the reader will be able to make certain connections between the *je* of the poem and the poet himself.

Much current critical interest in Villon's irony centers around two basic questions: Should we attempt to distinguish irony from authenticity in Villon's poetry? And what are the implications of Villon's ambiguity? This chapter, directed more toward the intended reader than his modern counterpart, revolves around a different critical axis: Does Villon's ambiguity reflect a devious intent, or does it reflect instead the state of alienation experienced by the uninitiated reader? And, if all Villon's irony is meant to be perceived, what expectations must be met by the reader?

Wayne Booth observes with characteristic clarity the collaborative and exclusionary aspects of successfully communicated irony:

> Whenever an author conveys to his reader an unspoken point, he creates a sense of collusion against all those, whether in the story or out of it, who do not get the point. Irony is always thus in part a device for excluding as well as for including, and those who are included, those who happen to have the necessary information to grasp the irony, cannot but derive at least part of their pleasure from a sense that others are excluded.[6]

In applying Booth's description of irony to Villon's work, I will focus on three phrases that I find especially relevant to the subject at hand. By manipulating irony, the author "creates a sense of collusion." The word "collusion" carries clear connotations of malicious intent, and the device of irony, especially in Villon's work, can be seen as a tacit contract, uniting author and reader in a fraudulent design, a cooperative deceit. Like the jargon of the *Coquillards,* the secret language with which Villon experimented in several of his poems, the irony of the *Testament* protects the author's actual meaning from being understood by the unini- tiated reader. Insofar as we are able to decipher the poet's true meaning, thanks to the minimal information we possess concern- ing certain individuals mentioned in the poem as well as obvious patterns of ironic discourse that may be observed by any percep- tive reader, we are able, albeit in a fairly limited manner, to share a sense of collusion with the author or perhaps, more accurately, to vicariously share the collusion between Villon and his intended reader. When Villon speaks of his three poor orphans, for ex- ample, we know for certain that the individuals to whom he refers are neither poor nor young:

> Item, j'ay sceu en ce voyaige
> Que mes troys povres orphelins
> Sont creuz et deviennent an aage
> Et n'ont pas testes de belins. (1274–1277)

> [Item on this trip I learned
> That my three piteous orphans
> Have grown up and come of age
> And aren't thick-skulled at all.]

We are able to penetrate the surface of the text because past read- ing experience has taught us that Villon's legatees are normally subject to antiphrastic description and because the verses consti- tute an intertextual reference to a passage of the *Lais* in which the three orphans are mentioned for the first time:

> Povres orphelins inpourveuz
> Tous deschaussez, tous despourveuz,
> Et desnuez comme le ver. (196–198)

> [Poor defenseless orphans
> Without shoes or clothes
> Bare as the worm.]

The "orphans" are then specifically identified as three individuals whom we know from archival evidence to have been wealthy, elderly contemporaries of the poet: Colin Laurens, Girart Gossouyn, and Jean Marceau. Our ability to perceive the irony of the reference to the "troys povres orphelins," then, derives from the fact that we "happen to have the necessary information to grasp the irony." The "necessary information" is the most critical element in the communication of irony, for without it the reader is unable to make certain connections that are vital to understanding the author's true intent. The information on which a reader draws may include not only factual data (name recognition, intertextual references, etc.) but also a subjective knowledge relating to the work of the author, a "feel" for the author's intention on which the reader relies to intuitively separate irony from authenticity. I will further explore the implications of this subjective knowledge as a criterion for identifying irony.

A final phrase from Booth's commentary merits reflection. Irony, he explains, consists essentially of an implied message communicated beneath the surface of the text as the "author conveys to his reader an unspoken point." Hence, perhaps more than any other literary device, irony maximizes reader participation. If a reliable narrator, to borrow Booth's terminology, is describing a beautiful and virtuous woman, the reader may passively accept the description as an honest portrayal and allow himself to uncritically assimilate the image that the author is attempting to evoke through the text. If, on the other hand, the reader senses that the description is a travesty perpetrated by an unreliable narrator (Villon's description of the *Grosse Margot*, for example), then he cannot passively acquiesce to the authority of the text if he wishes to grasp the author's actual intent and ultimately decipher the unwritten message. Instead, he must rely on all the relevant information at his disposal, tap all his "sources," and make all the right connections. The perception of irony, then, far from being either a random or passive process, makes very specific and possibly even exigent demands upon the reader.

Wolfgang Iser speaks of "blanks" in the text that the reader is obliged to fill in.[7] Iser reminds us that the act of reading requires attention not only to what is in the text but also to what has been omitted: "He [the reader] is drawn into the events and made to supply what is meant from what is not said. What is said only appears to take on significance as a reference to what is not said; it is the implications and not the statements that give shape and weight to the meaning."[8] The modern reader is hampered by his inability to fill in all the blanks or even to determine where all the blanks exist.

Virtually all readers would agree that elements of self-mockery as well as genuine self-characterization exist in the *Testament;* there is little consensus, however, on the criteria by which one may be distinguished from the other. Some readers and critics, perhaps motivated more by frustration than reason, have concluded that Villon is a "slippery" poet who takes malicious delight in eluding the reader, constantly concealing his true intention beneath layers of ambiguity. This conclusion, understandable though it may be to anyone who has spent hours wrestling with Villon without ever succeeding in pinning him down, is based on the fallacy of confusing result with intent. The ambiguity that unquestionably exists for us did not necessarily exist for the intended reader. This is not to suggest that the original audience was unaware of equivocal statements in the poem. Indeed, it is reasonable to assume that the first public was even more aware and appreciative of the nuances of Villon's equivocality than we are today. But, although we are admittedly at a loss to confidently identify the tone of voice associated with the most personal passages of the *Testament*—those passages containing remarks related to self-perception, whether genuine or ironic—the intended reader was both equipped and expected to perceive the true sense of the statement.[9]

Practically all of these passages are clustered in the prologue of the poem, occurring within the first three hundred verses. One group of references centers around Villon's self-portrayal as a penitent sinner, belonging to what Stephen Nichols terms the "penitential voice" of the poem.[10] In the passage quoted earlier in the chapter Villon squarely acknowledges his sinful nature: "Je suis pecheur, je le sçay bien" (105). The word *pecheur* occurs again about two hundred verses later: "Il n'appartient a moy, pecheur" (294). In a parenthetical comment, reminiscent of Christ's injunction against passing judgment on others, he states:

> Je ne suis juge ne commis
> Pour pugnir n'assouldre meffait:
> De tous suis le plus imparfait;
> Loué soit le doulx Jhesu Crist! (259–262)

> [I'm no judge nor a deputy
> For pardoning or punishing wrongs
> I'm the most imperfect of all
> Praised be the mild Jesus Christ!]

Is Villon to be taken at his word? If so, these confessions of sin should be taken as genuinely expressing contrition and establishing a confessional tone while at the same time universalizing the condition of the author. If the word *pecheur* is used truthfully, does it reflect a Christian awareness of the human condition or rather refer implicitly to specific sins—the murder of Philippe Sermoise, the Navarre theft, and other dark episodes of which we are unaware? Or is the confession of sin undercut by a gentle touch of irony? Is the *mea culpa* recited with a smile? Is the poet simply putting on another mask for the amusement of his audience? Another possibility is that each of the three "confessions" carries a different connotation, according to its context. Thus, we may be witnessing an act of genuine contrition in one instance and a skillful but discernible counterfeit in another.

In judging the tone of each passage and weighing the confession of sin, the intended reader is able to rely on extratextual information that bears directly or indirectly on his reading. He may, for instance, recall certain specific occurrences of the word *pecheur* in Villon's conversational discourse, with which a given textual use of the word coincides or contrasts. If the word has a fairly regular connotation in spoken use by the author, it would be difficult for the reader to entirely dissociate that connotation from the written appearance of the same word. It is even quite possible that in the "confessional" passages the reader might recognize entire phrases that he has already heard the poet use in private exchanges. The reader may also rely on his knowledge of Villon's attitude toward past transgressions, that is, whether their memory inspires humor, boasting, indifference, remorse, or reticence. If Villon is not merely referring to original sin but speaking instead of certain specific sins, the reader will be familiar, perhaps even a coparticipant, with many of these events. Personally acquainted with both the sinner and the sin, he will automatically make an informed judgment concerning the authenticity of the "penitential voice."

Another series of passages centers around the poet's past. Hardships and suffering, Villon claims, have sharpened his understanding of the world far more effectively than his formal education:

> Or est vray qu'aprés plains et pleurs
> Et angoisseux gemissemens,
> Aprés tritresses et douleurs,
> Labeurs et griefz cheminemens,
> Travail mes lubres sentemens,
> Esguisez comme une pelocte,
> M'ouvrist plus que tous les commens
> D'Averroÿs sur Arristote. (89–96)

> [It's true that after laments
> And tears and groans of anguish
> After sadnesses and sorrows
> Hard labor and bitter days on the road
> Suffering unlocked my tangled feelings
> About as sharp as a ball of wool
> More than all the *Commentaries*
> of Averroës and Aristotle.]

Is the stanza inspired by fresh memories of imprisonment, including recollections of physical and mental torture? Has the man who returned from the ecclesiastical prison been profoundly affected by the experience, as he claims? If the trauma to which he refers has in fact opened his *sentemens*, his mind, is this transformation evident to those who knew him before the experience? I do not mean by this series of questions to necessarily cast doubt on the reality of the suffering, its intensity, or the extent to which it affected the man who recalls it here. My personal inclination, one shared by many readers of Villon, is to accept the declaration as one firmly grounded on actual experience.

Many other readers will claim that the passage represents an exaggeration, if not a distortion, of the truth and that it ought to be taken no more seriously than any of the patently ironic passages of the poem. Again, the modern reader arrives at an impasse. Unlike the intended reader, we are incapable of judging whether the litany of sufferings—*plains, pleurs, gemissements, tritresses, douleurs, labeurs, cheminemens, travail*—reflects an honest appraisal of several painful experiences, whether it parodies a series of fairly trivial misfortunes by magnifying them to epic proportions or whether hyperbole and memories of intense suffering are somehow combined in the passage. If Villon intends the passage to be taken with any degree of seriousness, he depends on his reader to connect the text to stories of actual experiences recounted by the victim himself. If he intends the verses to be read with any degree of irony, he depends on his reader's ability to contrast the actual experiences with their manner of presentation. Either way, an informed reading of the text requires both a knowledge of the events to which it alludes and an awareness of the poet's attitude toward these events.

At various points in the *Testament* the poet portrays himself as a man separated from his youth. These passages are problematic to the reader who has no basis on which to ascertain the tone of the speaker. How, for example, are we to read the following excerpt?

> Je plains le temps de ma jeunesse,
> Ouquel j'ay plus qu'autre gallé

Jusqu'a l'entree de viellesse,
Qui son partement m'a cellé. (169–172)

[I mourn the days of my youth
When more than most I had my fling
Until age came upon me
It gave no warning it would leave.]

That a thirty-year-old man could find himself so far removed
from youth may seem to many readers a patent exaggeration.
These readers will see the characterization as another example of
self-parody, old age being merely a different mask taken from the
poet's repertoire. Given medieval standards of longevity, however, it is perfectly conceivable that a man entering his fourth
decade of life would feel he had crossed the threshold separating
youth and old age, especially if, as is the case in this passage, the
human lifespan is divided exclusively into these two broad do-
mains. Again, the perception of the author's intent requires an
awareness of his personality that transcends the textual evidence.

The same applies to the note of regret, whether genuine or
fabricated, expressed in the following conjecture:

Bien sçay, se j'eusse estudïé
Ou temps de ma jeunesse folle
Et a bonnes meurs dedïé,
J'eusse maison et couche molle. (201–204)

[Ah God if only I had studied
In the days of my heedless youth
And set myself in good ways
I'd have a house now and soft bed.]

The passage contains no moral judgment; it condemns the mis-
spent youth on purely practical grounds, pointing out how the
author's present material condition results from decisions he
either made or failed to make in his past. To know how to read
the statement, one must know something of the poet's attitude
toward his economic situation. The *Testament,* to be sure, con-

tains numerous allusions to the writer's poverty, but these remarks offer little guidance to the reader attempting to uncover
the meaning of these particular verses. The degree of remorse
expressed in the passage ultimately hinges on the value the
speaker attaches to the *maison* and *couche molle*. Do they mean
enough to him to warrant the sacrifice implicit in trading a *jeunesse folle* for *bonnes meurs?* The familiar problem recurs. There are
passages of Villon's poetry to which we are virtually tone-deaf.

The personal sections of the *Testament* are almost always
linked to circumstantial information that cannot be recovered
from the text itself. In presenting his current economic situation,
for example, Villon refers to the lack of financial and moral support on the part of his relatives:

> Des miens le mendre, je dy voir,
> De me desavouer s'avance,
> Oubliant naturel devoir
> Par faulte d'un peu de chevance. (181–184)

> [The last of my kin I speak the truth
> Steps up to disown me
> Forgetting their natural duty
> For my lack of a little money.]

Given what we know of the various criminal charges that Villon
managed to collect by 1462 and the notorious reputation that
must have been growing from these repeated entanglements with
civil and ecclesiastical authorities, it is perfectly plausible that
the passage has some basis in truth. Whether the abandonment
described here is due to the poet's loss of social respectability or
lack of financial resources, as he claims, whether the passage represents an exaggeration, slight or severe, of an actual situation or
constitutes a complete fabrication intended to reinforce the image
of a hopeless victim is completely open to speculation—*our* speculation, of course. Only when interpreted against a background
of factual information, can the claim of truth, "je dy voir," be
properly evaluated. Villon is either demonstrating to his reader

that a voice of truth may be discerned running through this polyphonic work, or he is undercutting the impact of the following assertion by alerting the reader to the exaggeration or falsehood it contains. In either case, the phrase "je dy voir" can only meaningfully communicate authorial intent if read against a background of extratextual information.

Separating irony from truthfulness in the *Testament,* as in the common conversational discourse we hear every day, ultimately depends either on recognizing the speaker's tone of voice or in perceiving a contrast or correspondence between the speaker's statement and his actual attitude toward the subject of his comments. We all know the amusing experience of seeing individuals who are relatively unacquainted with a speaker take an ironic statement seriously or read sarcasm into an innocent remark, while the speaker's actual intention remains perfectly unambiguous for those who know him well. The successful perception of a basic truth underlying the speaker's discourse depends, in the end, on the listener's sensitivity. Changes of tone in the *Testament* can be fully perceived, and are meant to be fully perceived, only by the reader who is truly sensitive to the poet's voice, one who is equipped to judge the tonal quality of the voice by juxtaposing it with personal knowledge of the man to whom it is inextricably connected.

Some may argue that to tie the meaning of these passages to extratextual information available only to a tiny circle of original readers unjustifiably invalidates any effort at critical interpretation. To this objection I answer that any critical approach, whatever its merits, is subject to certain limitations. Contemporary criticism, for all its diversity, strengths, and interdisciplinary breadth, often seems to function on a positivist assumption that all texts will yield their profoundest meaning, provided the right analytical technique is applied with adequate perseverance. Although much of the *Testament* has been elucidated by the penetrating insights of numerous critics, there are risks in subjecting certain portions of the poem to excessive interpretive pressure, in effect "forcing the text." Speculation is arguably the duty of the critic when faced with irresolvable meanings, and speculative activity need not be reckless and arbitrary but responsible. Still, the most productive line of approach to certain passages of the *Testament* may be to place less emphasis on deciphering the message, on "cracking the code," and to focus instead on the patterns of author/reader interaction that these passages imply. Critical response to Villon's poetry need not be limited to exercises in literary cryptography.

4
patterns of interaction

In the case of imagery and irony, reader participation, despite its importance, takes subtle and unobtrusive forms. The role of the reader, however, is not always inconspicuous. The *Testament* cannot be considered in its entirety without substantial attention to the reader's role, for the author's awareness of the reader, whether verbalized or implicit, becomes a major cohesive element of the poem, contributing greatly to its structural unity. Throughout the work the reader's presence is repeatedly acknowledged, sometimes with dramatic emphasis, sometimes by indirect suggestion. Partially shaped around the participation of the reader as one of the poem's dramatis personae, the *Testament* often functions as a dialogue more than a monologue. Although the reader's verbal responses to the poet's remarks are more often implied than explicitly expressed, they still influence the speaker's discourse, as he reacts, repeats, anticipates, argues, and explains in response to the presence of the reader.

The interaction of the author and the reader in the *Testament* is by no means a predictably mechanical process but rather a complex and dynamic relationship, generating humor, irony, and a variety of dramatic effects. The relationship, although based on certain expectations concerning the intended reader, is at least partially accessible to any reader of the poem. Indeed, it would be difficult for anyone reading the work to entirely avoid the various means by which Villon "baits" his reader. The term "reader," while continuing to designate Villon's intended reader, will also extend generically to all readers in cases where the reader's role does not strictly depend on personal acquaintance with the poet and his milieu.

The *Testament* is comprised of various linguistic registers, to borrow Paul Zumthor's terminology, each utilizing a specific type of language associated with a distinct social, literary, or religious function.[1] Elements of legal, courtly, and liturgical language, for example, may be found scattered through the work. The dominant register, however, is not connected to any specific sphere of intellectual or cultural activity. The mode of expression chosen with far greater frequency than any other is that of conversational discourse. Villon excels at creating the impression of a relaxed, spontaneous flow of words, punctuated by the various disruptions, hesitancies, and digressions that characterize natural speech. In a typical transition, the speaker prepares to move from one topic of conversation to another:

> Laissons le moustier ou il est,
> Parlons de chose plus plaisante;
> Ceste matiere a tous ne plest,
> Ennuieuse est et desplaisante. (265–268)

> [Let's forget all that
> And talk of something more pleasant
> Not everyone enjoys the topic
> It's dreary and unpleasant.]

The use of the first person plural in the first two verses implies the presence of a silent listener, and the verb *parlons* suggests the possibility of a conversational exchange, even though the speaker clearly dominates the conversation at the moment. The second half of the passage offers not only an explanation for the change of topic but also an apparent apology to the listener. In any case, the phrase "Ceste matiere a tous ne plest" clearly implies an awareness of the listener/reader, as well as a concern, genuine or simulated, for any offense the previous topic may have caused. The thematic flow of the poem, then, is altered in response to a projected reaction of the reader. The sincerity of Villon's apparent delicacy, his reluctance to offend a reader who will eventually be subjected to all manner of obscenity and distasteful imagery, is, of course, subject to discussion. More important is the fact that the text evinces here an awareness of the reader, of the reader's capacity to react, and ascribes a change of topic to the reader's presence. Thus, the reader at the outset of the poem is seemingly empowered to exercise restraint over the poet. By the same token, the poet acknowledges the central role of the reader, who, by reacting to the speaker, influences the course of the poem.

Following the familiar pattern of a speaker conscious of his listener's attention, the poet often digresses, interrupts, or corrects himself, appears to hesitate and think aloud:

> Qu'avoir esté seigneur . . . Que dis?
> Seigneur, lasse! ne l'est il mais? (289–290)

> [Having once been a lord . . . What am I saying?
> Alas, isn't he a lord still?]

> Qui luy portera? Que je voye . . .
> Ce sera Pernet de la Barre (936–937)

> [Who'll deliver it? Let me think . . .
> Make it Perrenet of the Bar]

> Item, a Thibault de la Garde . . .
> Thibault? je mens: il a nom Jehan. (1354–1355)

> [Item to Thibault de la Garde . . .
> Thibault? I'm kidding, his name is Jean.]

The disrupted speech flow, which Rychner indicates by the editorial insertion of suspension points, results in a momentary silence. The poetic discourse, like any extended act of improvised speech, is punctuated by brief pauses allowing the speaker time to reflect and possibly modify a preceding statement. These silences in the poem are associated with a certain self-consciousness as the speaker utilizes the disjunctive pauses to create a variety of dramatic effects by exploiting and heightening the reader's attention.

Overall, the speech patterns of the *Testament* suggest a loquacious conversationalist who, although occasionally trying the patience of his listener, remains very much aware of his audience. One of the work's strongest tensions is produced by the opposition between the highly formalized nature of the legal will—its tendency to rigidify, codify, and legalize all language—and the loose rhythms and informal phrasing that characterize so much of Villon's poetic will. A second tension derives from the conflict between rigorous metrical constraints and the supple, natural language that operates within these restrictions. The poem succeeds in achieving a sense of flexibility and naturalness largely because the author remains aware of his reader's presence.

The speaker's discourse is frequently broken by a question that elicits a brief explanatory comment. Considering the case of once virtuous women who have become prostitutes, the poet is confronted with a question of causality:

> Qui les meut a ce? G'ymagine,
> Sans l'onneur des dames blasmer,
> Que c'est nature femeninne
> Qui tout unyement veult amer. (609–612)

> [What makes them do it? I imagine
> No offense meant to female honor
> Something in the nature of woman
> Makes them love many men at once.]

It is possible to take the question as an anticipation of the reader's skeptical reaction to the claim that these dishonored *fillectes* (590) were once *femmes honnestes* (592). The role assigned to the reader may be even more direct, for the question may also be read as an actual interruption by the latter. In this case the text, by echoing the interlocutor's question, admits a new voice into the poem. The initial reaction to the question—"G'ymagine . . ."—supports this interpretation, for the speaker gives the impression of improvising a speculative answer to a perplexing question that has caught him somewhat off guard.

Appointing his executors toward the end of the poem, Villon begins by naming Martin Bellefoye, but before he can name the second he is interrupted by his impatient reader:

> C'est maistre Mertin Bellefoye,
> Lieutenant du cas criminel.
> Qui sera l'autre? G'y pensoye:
> Ce sera sire Colombel. (1928–1931)

> [One is master Martin Bellafaye
> Lieutenant of criminal cases
> Who's next? Hmmm, let's see
> Make it Sire Colombel.]

Again a reflective comment—"G'y pensoye"—gives the impression of a slight delay while an answer to the unexpected question is being formulated.

The interrogative remarks that punctuate the poem are not, for the most part, lengthy rhetorical questions but brief, pointed interruptions, consisting of a short phrase or even a single word, eliciting a retraction, clarification, or expansion of a preceding statement:

> Si vueil qu'ilz voisent a l'estude;
> Ou? Sur maistre Pierre Richier. (1282–1283)

> [So I want them to enter school
> Where? At master Pierre Richer's.]

The insertion of the one-word question, disrupting the rhythm of the discourse, signals an intrusion into the the speaker's train of thought or at least a momentary disarticulation. The abrupt question forces a minimal pause into the text, sharpening the relief of the subsequent answer.

In echoing the reader's questions, Villon employs a construct that Walker Gibson terms the "mock reader."[2] The reader with whom he is dialectically engaged, whose questions, doubts, challenges continually manifest themselves, is to some degree a product of the author's imagination. Still, one must remember that the purpose of a mock reader is to draw the actual reader into a text, encouraging him to identify with his appointed representative. Thus, the valid questions logically connected to preceding statements that periodically interrupt the speaker become our questions, as we allow our role to merge with that of the mock reader. One may even argue, with some justification, that the mock reader of the *Testament* is not a purely fictional character devoid of resemblance to the intended reader but rather a composite of the author's expectations of his specific audience.

In the evolving dialogue of the *Testament,* questions pass not only from reader to author but in the opposite direction as well:

> Ou sont les gracïeux galans
> Que je suivoye ou temps jadiz,
> Si bien chantans, si bien parlans,
> Sy plaisans en faiz et en diz? (225–228)

> [Where are the happy young men
> I ran with in the old days
> Who sang so well, who spoke so well
> So excellent in word and deed?]

Unlike the *ubi sunt* questions of the "Ballade des dames du temps jadis," relating to figures of myth and legend, the question here pertains to actual persons known to the poet. For the reader able to connect the *gracieux galans* with mutual acquaintances, or at least with some knowledge of Villon's past associations, the question differs from the series of purely rhetorical questions contained in the trilogy of ballades to follow. The question, then, personalizes the *ubi sunt* theme while at the same time reinforcing the private bond that joins the poet to his reader.

Queries to the reader, although not always open-ended,

generally invite him to formulate an answer or perhaps to choose from several possible answers. Thus, the reader is literally asked to respond to the text. Summarizing the points of Franc Gontier's philosophy with which he disagrees, Villon asks the reader to judge the *debat:*

> Mais en ce debat cy nous sommes,
> Car il loue sa pouvreté,
> Estre povre yver et esté,
> Et a felicité reppute
> Ce que tiens a maleurté.
> Lequel a tort? Or en discute. (1467–1472)

> [In fact, the reason we've fallen to arguing
> Is that he boasts about his poverty
> How he's poor winter and summer
> And ascribes to happiness
> The things that belong to misery
> Who's in the wrong? I argue as follows.]

The question "Lequel a tort?" casts the reader in the role of arbitrator, requiring that he listen to the debate (of which he will hear only one side), weigh the "evidence," and then render a judgment. Not only in this passage but throughout much of the *Testament* the reader is implicitly asked to hear the "defendant's" case, to consider the arguments, and to eventually reach a judgment, which, given the biased nature of the presentation, can only be in favor of the "accused."

Questions in the *Testament* obviously constitute more than a mere stylistic device. Any question, even if rhetorical, is directed to an audience and implies the speaker's awareness of that audience. Passing back and forth from the author to the reader, and from the reader (through the intermediary of the mock reader) to the author, questions open and maintain channels of cross-communication. At the very least, they establish the author's recognition of his audience, an awareness that endows his poem with a slightly self-conscious character. Whether boasting, jus-

tifying himself, mocking his failures, attacking his personal enemies, or simply entertaining with panache, the poet evinces a
continual cognizance of his reader's presence.

The relationship between Villon and his reader constantly
fluctuates. As already demonstrated, the reader may be cast in
the role of a silently supportive listener, an impatient, curious,
or skeptical interlocutor, a sympathetic judge. At times the relationship becomes a dialectical encounter, as the author defends
himself against an anticipated objection from the reader. Early in
the poem the author momentarily takes an adversarial stance,
preparing to parry an attack. Having opened the poem with bitter words against Thibaut d'Aussigny, the poet foresees a possible
objection to the harsh verbal treatment of his former captor:

> Et s'aucun me vouloit reprendre
> Et dire que je le maudiz,
> Non faiz, se bien me scet comprendre;
> En riens de luy ne mesdiz. (17–20)

> [If someone wants to object
> And say I'm cursing the man
> I'm not if you see my meaning
> I don't speak ill of him at all.]

The deceptive simplicity of these verses conceals a rather complex
network of relationships between the author and the reader. The
objection anticipated on the part of the reader, designated at this
and other points in the poem by the indeterminate *aucun,* can
hardly be taken as a challenge worthy of serious consideration.
The anger against Thibaut d'Aussigny vented in the first two
stanzas of the poem is, from the poet's point of view at least, so
justified that the imagined reproach clearly has no validity. Thus,
the poet engages in a playful debate with his reader, anticipating
a humorous objection (i.e., "How can you say such nasty things
about this poor guy?") and answering with a humorous rebuttal
(i.e., "Me? Never! I even pray for him").

It is also possible to interpret *aucun* not as one of the poet's intended readers but as a hypothetical, uninitiated reader outside the small circle, whom Villon inserts into the poem at this point for the amusement of his privileged audience.[3] This misplaced reader, whose naive reprimand manifests an exaggerated sense of morality, a saintly piety, or a blind respect for established authority, attempts to come to the bishop's rescue and becomes himself the butt of the poet's sarcasm. Thus, the rebuke is answered with a flat lie that, one assumes, will satisfy the naive detractor. The bishop's defender, who has somehow wandered into the *Testament*, serves to solidify the bond connecting the author to his intended reader, demonstrating the estrangement of the uninitiated reader who is thrust into a very private and alien world.

Villon's reply to the anticipated objection contains a crucial clue to the reader, revealing something about both the nature of the text and the posture the reader should assume toward the text. He emphatically claims that he is not cursing the bishop and states that his intent will be clear to anyone who has a proper understanding of the matter ("Non faiz, se bien me scet comprendre"). Galway Kinnell gives a free translation of the verse, which, although taking some liberties with the literal meaning of the line, renders well the gist of the statement: "I'm not if you see my meaning."[4] The affirmation of truthfulness in the face of a blatant lie opens to question the entire discourse of the poem. At the same time, a certain rapport is being built between the author and the reader, a rapport posited on the understanding that truth is discernible to the reader who "knows how to understand." In effect, the author is demonstrating to his reader that: (1) the text does not always mean what it says; (2) a naive reading can lead to a misreading; and (3) the comprehension of the author's meaning requires a special knowledge on the part of the reader. The pathetic confusion of the innocent reader results precisely from his "illiteracy" when confronted with this particular text. However, to interpret Villon's message to the reader as an indication that all statements in the poem are necessarily equivocal would, for the reasons cited earlier, create a distortion that would often lead to misinterpretation.

Another anticipated accusation concerns the slander not of an actual individual but of the mythic figure of *Amour*. Having completed a lengthy tirade against love, Villon imagines a possible protest:

> Et s'aucun m'interrogue ou tente
> Comment d'Amours j'ose mesdire,
> Ceste parolle le contente:
> "Qui meurt a ses loix de tout dire." (725–728)

> [And if anyone steps up and asks
> What right I have to abuse love so
> Let him make do with this answer
> A dying man should have his say.]

As in the case of the earlier confrontation, the argument may represent the playful intrusion of a friendly reader, feigning dismay at Villon's harsh treatment of love. The false offense is answered with a false excuse: "Qui meurt a ses loix de tout dire." It is equally plausible to connect the protest to another innocent reader, or perhaps the same one who naively attempted to defend Thibaut d'Aussigny. In this case, the reader's dismay results from Villon's flagrant violation of the courtly code, his blasphemous disrespect for the love-lord. The verb *oser* ("Comment d'Amours j'ose mesdire") underlines the enormity of the transgression in the eyes of the protester. Rather than deny the charge, the poet accepts it this time, implying that his proximity to death justifies even the most outrageous profanity.

The verbal confrontations are occasionally rendered more explicit, as the voice of the mock reader actually enters the poem. Attempting to persuade the poet not to renounce love despite his disillusionment with the easily corruptible nature of feminine virtue, the protesting voice points out what he perceives as the fallacy of the speaker's argument:

Et qui me vouldroit laidanger
De ce mot, en disant: "Escoute!
Se d'amer t'estrange et reboute
Le barrat de celles nommees,
Tu faiz une bien folle doubte,
Car ce sont femmes diffamees." (571–576)

[But suppose someone wants to challenge me
For these remarks saying "Listen
If you're disgusted, thrown off love
By the slippery dealings of the ones you've named
Your misgiving is nonsense
For these are women of ill repute."]

The objection comes not from a stranger, the naive reader who has wandered into the *Testament,* but from someone who knows the poet well enough to use the *tu* form of address. The intimacy of the relationship is further underscored by the natural, unpretentious manner in which the listener interrupts the speaker with a note of impatience and urgency—"Escoute!"—an exclamation still used today among close acquaintances making similar interruptions. Without a trace of the moral indignation that colors the defense of love and Thibaut d'Aussigny, the voice gently chides the poet for succumbing to foolish fears: "Tu faiz une bien folle doubte." Rather than an attack, the objection represents a firm but sympathetic desire to disabuse the poet, to "talk some sense" into him.

The voice continues by elaborating on the fickleness of the *femmes diffamees* and concludes with these words of advice:

Mais en femmes d'onneur et nom
Franc homme, se Dieu me sequere,
Se doit emploier, ailleurs non. (582–584)

[An upright man so help me God
Should take up with women
Of good reputation and with no others.]

67

Without entirely contradicting the impression of a friendly objection, the concluding comment opens the possibility of an ironic intention. The suggestion that the poet adopt the conduct of an upright man, a *franc homme,* and seek the company of *femmes d'onneur* can easily be taken as a tongue-in-cheek remark. The injection of moral terms into an inappropriate context effectively undercuts the pretense of urgent concern present at the outset of the interruption. At the same time, far from casting suspicion on the friendly nature of the intrusion, the final ironic twist only reinforces the intimacy of the relationship while evincing a sense of humor totally absent in the reaction of the innocent reader.

Whether serious or ironic, the argument becomes a straw man for Villon, who characteristically has the last word in the matter:

> Je prens qu'aucun dye cecy,
> Sy ne me contente il en rien.
> En effect, il conclud ainsi,
> Et je le cuide entendre bien,
> Qu'on doit amer en lieu de bien. (585–589)

> [Let's say someone tells me that
> He doesn't impress me one bit
> In effect he draws the conclusion
> If I understand his meaning well
> You should love only in good circles.]

He concludes by claiming that the distinction between honorable and dishonorable women is meaningless, since all prostitutes were once *femmes honnestes* (592). As a stylistic device, the little debate serves a number of functions, creating humor by the juxtaposition of love and prostitution and also relieving the monotony of a single narrative voice, thus adding another rhetorical dimension to the work.

In sharp contrast to the familiar tone of the intervention just discussed, the other listener whose voice is heard in the poem expresses a very different attitude:

Qui me diroit: "Qui vous fait mectre
Si tres avant ceste parolle,
Qui n'estes en theologie maistre?
A vous est presumpcïon folle." (809–812)

[If someone should say "How can you
Speak out so brashly
When you're not even master of theology?
Your presumption is incredible."]

The use of *vous* immediately distances the interlocutor from the poet, distinguishing this voice from the one using the familiar form of address. The righteous indignation of the speaker is unmistakable. His insistence on the poet's lack of proper theological credentials, a lack which in the speaker's view disqualifies the poet from making any sound judgment on theological matters, betrays a greater respect for established authority than for native intellectual abilities. Again, a "righteous reader" is thrust into the private world of the *Testament* for the purpose of mockery and amusement.

The dialectical element of Villon's poetry, as Jean-Claude Muhlethaler observes, is reminiscent of rhetorical techniques employed in the sermons of Gerson and Courtecuisse and also parallels certain monologues of late medieval comic theater.[5] Odette Petit-Morphy points to a connection with the *dubitatio* and *disputatio* of medieval scholastic training.[6] Whatever their ultimate origins, the debates of the *Testament,* whether informal or structured, carry important implications for any serious study of the author/reader relationship in Villon's poetry. It must be recognized, of course, that the reader whose objections are represented or perhaps misrepresented, opposed, and ultimately disarmed or discredited cannot be accurately identified with the actual reader. Nevertheless, in these sections of the poem Villon is communicating with his actual reader through the device of the "dummy reader." By mocking the latter's inability to grasp the spirit of the text, Villon reminds the reader who "scet comprendre" to tread carefully through the labyrinth of the *Testament,* avoiding the snares laid for those who lose their bearings. In effect, Villon teaches his reader how to read the poem, by giving him several demonstrations of how *not* to read it.

Not all challenges take the form of an indignant protest, and many objections are countered without apparent malice. The source of these intrusions and the kind of attitude they represent are ultimately less important than the regularity of the intrusions themselves. Whether coming from friendly or hostile quarters, interruptions bombard the narrator with remarkable frequency. Consequently, a significant portion of the poem is devoted to resisting these incursions. Yet as each assault is turned back, another soon replaces it. The broad pattern that emerges from these repeated verbal skirmishes is that of an author interacting with his readers. Whether these readers are real or imaginary is ultimately of little importance, for the interaction dramatized within the text itself is a suggested model for the actual reading process. Following the example of the readers who variously manifest their presence in the poem, the actual reader is invited to question or challenge whenever he feels it appropriate. The fact that dialectical discourse is such a basic structural device in the *Testament* demonstrates that the text by its very nature opens itself to question. In this sense, the text demands a critical reading, in all senses of the adjective.

The author's awareness of the reader is manifested, among other ways, by a series of comments aimed directly or indirectly at the latter. These often take the form of asides to the reader. Ending a long digression and vaguely attempting to return to the matter at hand, the writing of the will, Villon recognizes the fact that he has wandered off his path:

> En cest incident me suis mis,
> Qui de riens ne sert a mon fait. (257–258)

> [I've gone into this story
> which adds nothing to my purpose.]

The resolve to stick to his subject fails repeatedly, and another half-hearted apology follows about five hundred verses later:

> Somme, plus ne diray q'un mot,
> Car commencer vueil a tester. (777–778)
>
> [Now I'll add just one more word
> For I'm eager to start on the will.]

Other asides come in the form of explanatory insertions clarifying a bequest:

> Item, aux Unze Vings sergens
> ....
> J'entends a ceulx a pié, hohecte! (1086, 1092)
>
> [*Item* to the Eleven-twenty Sergeants
> ....
> I mean the foot patrol of course]
>
> Item, pour ce que le seelleur
> ....
> J'entends celluy de l'Eveschié. (1198, 1204)
>
> [*Item* because the Keeper of the Seal
> ....
> I mean the one who serves the bishop.]

Realizing the possibility of misconstruction, Villon adds an exegetical comment for the benefit of the reader. The explanatory phrase in each case implicitly acknowledges a potential misreading and serves as another cue to the reader to pay attention to the author's *entente*.

The concern with interpretation and misinterpretation is implied in other passages as well. In an intertextual reference Villon comments on the title that his first poetic will, composed six years earlier, has now acquired:

Sy me souvient bien, Dieu mercis,
Que je feiz a mon partement
Certains laiz, l'an cinquante six,
Qu'aucuns, sans mon consentement,
Voulurent nommer testament;
Leur plaisir fut, non pas le myen.
Mais quoy! on dit communement
Qu'ung chacun n'est maistre du scien. (753–760)

[I haven't forgotten, thank God
That when I went away in fifty-six
I composed certain legacies
That some without my consent
Were determined to call a testament
This was their idea not mine
But so what? As they say
No one is master of his own.]

The work, never formally titled by its author, is designated both in the poem itself and in the passage quoted above as a *lais*.[7] Once released to the public, it not only acquired a title but a title that the author considers inappropriate and emphatically rejects. Still, the tone of resignation apparent in the last two verses implies the stoic acceptance of an unalterable situation. The circle of readers in which the *Lais* circulated undoubtedly overlapped the *Testament*'s immediate circle, possibly to a large extent, and the fate of the first poem thus bears on the reading of the second. The passage tacitly acknowledges the possibility for distortion inherent in any act of interpretation. The readers of the *Lais* have in effect expanded the original text with the gratuitous addition of a title, and in so doing they have not only violated the author's intention, but—given the primacy of any title as a clue to the significance of a literary work—measurably altered the meaning of the poem. The ramifications for the *Testament* are clear. If the reader tampers with the text in any way, he will inevitably be imposing his own order on the work, thus partially depriving it of its original meaning.

At the same time, the title that has been imposed on the

earlier poetic will demonstrates the process by which a text evolves through interaction with the reader and how powerless the author is to control this evolution. Toward the end of the *Testament,* Villon gives his notary, Jehan Calais, unlimited authority to construe and even modify the document at his discretion:

> De le gloser et commenter,
> De le diffinir et descripre,
> Diminuer ou augmenter,
> De le canceller et perscripre
> De sa main, et ne sceut escripre,
> Interpreter et donner sens
> A son plaisir, meilleur ou pire,
> A tout cecy je m'y consens. (1852–1859)

> [To gloss and annotate it
> To define and clarify it
> To shorten or lengthen it
> To void it and scratch it out
> With his own hand and if he can't write
> To interpret and make sense of it
> For better or worse as he likes
> To all the above I do here consent.]

Without crediting Villon with prophetic powers enabling him to predict the critical scrutiny to which his text would be subjected during the five centuries following its composition, one may reasonably read the passage as a commentary on the vulnerability of the written word. Reading, as an interpretative act, always entails the risk that the author's meaning will be distorted or misconstrued. Villon again subtly reminds his reader of the potential gap between intent and interpretation and produces, albeit unintentionally, a remarkably apt description of the reading process:

> Interpreter et donner sens
> A son plaisir, meilleur ou pire. (1857–1858)

> [To interpret and make sense of it
> For better or worse as he likes.]

Rather than Jehan Calais, an individual whom Villon admits he has never met, the intended reader is accurately described by the phrase applied to the former: "Pour ce que scet bien mon entente" (1844). The greatest risk of misinterpretation will come when the poem is no longer confined to its original readership, although even these first readers, as they have proven in their mishandling of the *Lais,* are capable of inflicting unintended damage on the text.

The relationship between the author and the reader is sometimes based on alliance rather than opposition. The two are bound together by certain commonalities, especially those of a religious nature:

> Et l'Eglise nous dit et compte
> Que prions pour noz annemys. (29–30)
>
> [But the Church asks and expects us
> To pray for our enemies.]

With the shift from the first person singular to the first person plural, Villon momentarily universalizes his personal situation. The personal enemy, Thibaut d'Aussigny, is now subsumed with all other enemies into the collective category (*noz annemys*) while the poet is subsumed within the broad *nous,* which expands to cover not only all readers but, transcending historical and cultural restrictions, extends to all Christians, to all those whose lives are under the direction and responsibility of the Church. The passage, then, establishes a certain solidarity between the author and his reader, implying that having enemies is part of the human condition.

The use of the first person plural in the *Testament* is almost always linked to an awareness of mortality:

> Ce monde n'est perpetuel,
> Quoy que pense riche pillart;
> Tous sommes soubz mortel coustel. (421–423)

[The world won't last forever
Whatever the robber baron may think
The mortal knife hangs over us all.]

It is significant that, although the alliance between author and
reader takes many forms throughout the poem, when this alliance is formally recognized by the first person plural, the bond
is based not on a private understanding but on acknowledgment
of the human condition. At these junctures, the privileged relationship between the author and the initiated reader is swallowed
by a vast, all-encompassing relationship that unites all human
lives in the face of imminent death.

Beyond the threat of death, the threat of judgment universalizes the medieval experience of Christianity, and the theme of
judgment—human, but especially divine—is very much in evidence in the poem. Referring to the story of Lazarus and the rich
man condemned to hell, Villon concludes by recognizing that
not only the rich are at risk of eternal damnation:

Puis que boiture y est si chiere,
Dieux nous garde de la main mise! (823–824)

[Because of the high price of liquor
God keep us from this, joking aside.]

The *nous* of this passage and of the passages cited immediately
prior to it might aptly be termed the "Christian *nous*." It reap-
pears at the end of the "Ballade pour prier Notre Dame":

Le Tout Puissant, prenant nostre foiblesse,
Laissa les cieulx et nous vint secourir. (905–906)

[Lord Almighty who took on our weakness
Left heaven and came down to save us.]

The Christian *nous* unites the author and reader as *frères humains*
among all human brothers of all time. In contrast to the author-

75

reader "contract" of the *Testament* that ties the meaning of the text to the knowledge of a specific context, severely restricted both spatially and chronologically, the spiritual fraternity of the Christian *nous* transcends all temporal bounds.[8] The opposition between these two relationships—the particular and the universal—derives not from the introduction of a separate category of readers opposing the intended audience but from a momentary enlargement of perspective in which poet and reader alike lose their distinguishing identity, as they are encompassed by a reality in which time, place, and personal differences are rendered meaningless.

Incursions of eternity inevitably yield to secular concerns as the temporal perspective closes again. Exploiting the fiction of the will, Villon orders his readers to carry out certain provisions. They are instructed to explain to anyone who does not receive his designated inheritance that the direct heirs—Moreau, Provins, and Turgis—have claimed everything, even the deathbed itself:

> De moy, dictes que je leur mande,
> Ont eu jusq'au lit ou je gis. (775–776)

> [Who from me, you can say I said so
> Got everything down to the bed I'm on.]

He facetiously orders his readers to pray for the soul of Michault "le Bon Fouterre" (923) and adds an equivocal phrase instructing that they go quickly to Michault's tomb or that they engage in the act whose abuse is supposed to have killed the legendary hero:

> Priés pour luy, faictes ung sault,
> A Sainct Sathur gist soubz Sancerre. (924–925)

> [Say a prayer for him, then go at it
> He lies at Saint-Satur below Sancerre.]

The "Ballade des femmes de Paris" is followed by a directive that the reader, addressed in the singular this time, personally observe the oratory skill of the *dames parisiennes* by surreptitiously approaching them while in church:

> Regarde m'en deux, troys assises
> Sur le bas du ply de leurs robes
> En ces moustiers, en ces eglises;
> Tire t'en pres et ne te hobes. (1543–1546)

> [I see them by twos and threes sitting
> With their skirts folded under them
> In these monasteries, these churches
> Draw near, don't make a sound.]

The reader who first encounters the *Grosse Margot* is instructed to recite to her the ballade composed in her honor:

> Qui la trouvera d'aventure,
> Qu'on lui lise ceste ballade. (1589–1590)

> [Whoever meets her on his rounds
> Is to read her this *ballade*.]

The final directive to the readers is that they recite (in unison, presumably) the requiem prayer that Villon has written for himself:

> Pour Dieu, dictes en ce verset:
> Repoz eternel donne a cil,
> Sire, et clarté perpetuelle. (1891–1893)

> [Say *Amen* with this *rondeau*.
> Rest eternal grant him
> Lord and everlasting light.]

Within the narrative framework of the *Testament,* of course, all these orders are directed to the executors of the will and are to be respectfully carried out as the last wishes of a dying man. Beyond this obvious function, the instructions to the reader bear

77

certain deeper implications. They create a pretense of subservience, placing the reader-executor under the authority of the author-testator. The former executes the poet's will in two senses. First, his fictive function is to implement the provisions of the legal document. Second, in a literal sense, he carries out the poet's volition, consummates the intent simply by understanding it. The execution of the will, in fact, proves a remarkable analogue for the reading process, for both the will and the literary text can be carried out only if the author's intent is successfully "implemented." Both represent a latent volition that can only be actualized by the "executor." In the case of the *Testament*, the author's instructions constitute another recognition of the reader's contribution to the collaborative enterprise of the poem.

To properly understand the will, Villon's executor, unlike other executors, is expected to exercise discretion, knowing when to take the text to the letter and when to read between the lines. The reading of the *Testament* demands that the reader remain in a constant state of vigilance, always prepared to grasp what is left unsaid as well as what is spoken. Indeed, the poem often appears written in two languages: the verbal language that comprises the text itself and also the nonverbal language of gestures, smiles, winks, dramatic poses, a whole system of mime accentuating or undercutting the apparent meaning of the spoken discourse. Thus, even the silences of the poem are not actually silent; where the words end, communication continues wordlessly. At several points in the poem the author claims with apparent discretion to pass over a subject that is best left undisturbed. In the opening of the will proper he states that he has been spared the *fievre eufumere* (829) by divine providence and then alludes to other suffering that he has not had the good fortune to avoid:

> Mais d'autre dueil et perte amere
> Je me tais, et ansi commence. (831–832)

> [But of other sorrows and bitter loss
> I say nothing and so begin.]

Although a total silence on the subject would guarantee concealment of the thought, the pretended omission, on the contrary, draws attention to the personal suffering and invites the initiated reader to speculate on the specific nature of this *dueil* and *perte amere*. The same technique is used in describing the gift bequeathed to Guillaume Charruau:

> Item, donne a mon advocat,
> Maistre Guillaume Charüau,
> Quoy? que Marchant ot pour estat,
> Mon branc; je me taiz du fourreau. (1022–1025)

> [*Item* I give to my lawyer
> Master Guillaume Charrau
> My cutlass but not the sheath
> Never mind that Marchant got it first.]

The feigned delicacy of the "omission" contrasts sharply with the obvious obscenity of the allusion, whether *branc* and *fourreau* are taken in a sexual or a scatological sense. By pretending to discreetly repress a vulgar observation, Villon actually sets the allusion in full relief. As in the case of the previously cited passage, the verb *taire* becomes paradoxical, announcing rather than concealing the presence of a thought.

Just as the claim of silence can mask an observation, the claim of truthfulness can mask an obvious falsehood. After reminding his readers of the Christian teaching on charity toward one's enemies, the poet insists that he intends to conform to this teaching:

> Je vous diray que j'ay tort et honte
> Quoy qu'il m'aist fait, a Dieu remys. (31–32)

> [I'll reply "I'm wrong and ashamed
> Whatever he did being in God's hands."]

From the nature of the mock prayer described in the following stanza, it immediately becomes clear that Villon has no intention of forgiving his enemy. The direct address of the readers, "Je vous diray . . . ," establishes a tone of candor and confidentiality. The falseness of the statement that follows is so readily apparent that only the most naive reader could be misled. By associating the act of speech with deceit rather than truth, while simultaneously invoking the presence of the reader, Villon implies that future assertions of truthfulness are open to question, the counterfeit insistence of sincerity inserted into the following legacy, for example:

> Vache ne leur donne ne beuf,
> Car vachiers ne sont ne bouviers,
> Mais gans a porter espreviers,
> Ne cuidez pas que je me joue. (1048–1051)

> [Since they aren't cowherds or beefeaters
> I give them neither cow nor ox
> But men for carrying the falcons
> Don't think I'm joking.]

The parenthetical remark to the reader reminds him that the text cannot always be taken at face value, indicating the author's inclination to play with the truth, alternating veracity with falsehood.

Of all the devices Villon employs to engage his reader, perhaps the most fascinating is the use of acrostics. Four ballades of the *Testament* contain acrostic signatures: the "Ballade pour prier Notre Dame" (VILLON), "Ballade a s'amye" (FRANÇOIS, MARTHE), "Ballade pour Robert d'Estouteville" (AMBROISE), "Ballade de la Grosse Margot" (VILLON).[9] Like Villon's irony, antiphrasis, pretended omissions, and equivocal statements, these acrostics comprise a hidden message, literally buried in the text. The immediate context of the message, the stanzaic structure that underlies and conceals the secret sign, exists in a symbiotic relationship with the acrostic, each in a sense generating the other. Confronting this juxtaposition of two separate messages, the reader is forced to find a logical connection between the two.

The task of the reader is not necessarily to discover the inherent meaning of this juxtaposition but rather to interpret the relationship in such a way that the acrostic makes sense.

Jonathan Culler cogently summarizes the difference between "meaning" and "sense" as applied to literary interpretation:

> Indeed, the semiotic program may be better expressed by the concepts of "sense" and "making sense" than by the concept of "meaning," for while "meaning" suggests a property of a text (a text "has" meaning), and thus encourages one to distinguish an intrinsic (though perhaps ungraspable) meaning from the interpretation of readers, "sense" links the qualities of a text to the operations one performs upon it. A text can make sense and someone can make sense of a text. [10]

The attempt to make sense of a text and the effort to discover its meaning are not, of course, mutually exclusive, and the first process may naturally lead to the second. Contemporary critical approaches, however, tend to concentrate on interpretive operations and intelligibility rather than authorial intent. Few critics would debate the premise that Villon's acrostics represent a deliberate design rather than a purely gratuitous addition. The actual process by which one makes sense of a given acrostic, however, varies according to the reader. This latitude of interpretation would apply to the original audience as well as to subsequent readers, although the original audience was obviously far better equipped to recognize no longer discernible intratextual and extratextual connections.

The acrostic contained in the "Ballade pour prier Notre Dame" illustrates the complexities entailed in the interpretation of the "coded" signature:

> Vous portastes, digne Vierge, princesse,
> Jhesus regnant qui n'a ne fin ne cesse.
> Le Tout Puissant, prenant nostre foiblesse,
> Laissa les cieulx et nous vint secourir,
> Offrit a mort sa tres clere jeunesse.

81

Nostre Seigneur tel est, tel le confesse:
En ceste foy je veul vivre et mourir. (903–909)

[Virgin so worthy, princess, you bore
Jesus who reigns without end or limit
Lord Almighty who took on our weakness
Left heaven and came down to save us
Offering his precious youth to death
Now such is our Lord, such I acknowledge him
In this faith I want to live and die.]

Dismissing the possibility that the acrostic is a meaningless or-namental addition, an assumption that would be supported nei-ther by critical consensus nor by general semantic patterns in Villon's poetry, the reader is left with the task of relating the acrostic to the *envoi,* of "making sense" out of the juxtaposition.

Karl Uitti finds in the acrostic a feminine version of Villon's name—VILLONE—and considers this transformation signifi-cant.[11] David Kuhn points to the pattern of the *noms divins* con-tained in the acrostic.[12] Edelgard DuBruck, although not com-menting specifically on the acrostic, indicates the strong credal tones of the *envoi* to which Villon's name is attached.[13] I have suggested elsewhere that Villon's acrostic signature symbolically incorporates the poet into the text of his mother's prayer.[14] Whatever divergent philosophical interpretations may be found in the acrostic, the reader is clearly led to formulate some con-nection between the name, VILLON, and the text generating it.

Some editors of Villon's poetry set the acrostics in bold print to draw the reader's attention to their existence. This editorial modification dramatizes the question of primacy confronting the reader. Highlighted in bold print, the acrostic naturally domi-nates the text; it literally takes precedence over the text, as the reader is reminded that the acrostic name precedes the actual composition of the verses, which are in turn built on the name's vertical arrangement. Thus, the acrostic serves as the creative and structural pivot of the stanza, ordering and generating the text that grows around it. In this sense, the name acquires a privileged status entitling it to be interpreted as the primary poetic message; the verses of the stanza, forming the generative context of the acrostic and thus serving a supportive function, are then relegated to a secondary status. On the other hand, when not physically highlighted in the text, the acrostic remains hidden at first reading, appearing only during a subsequent reading as a kind of afterthought, a by-product of the text, reinforcing or echoing the poetic message. Thus, the status of the acrostic is problematic. Whatever importance the reader ultimately attaches to the hidden name, its mere presence clearly affects the reading of the text.

With the acrostic, Villon invites the reader to read his poetry, figuratively and literally, from different angles. It is possible, for example, to extract both vertical and linear readings of the stanza cited above, combining the acrostic and the refrain to form a "marginal" reading:

V

I

L

L

O

N

En ceste foy je veul vivre et mourir.

With the conjunction of the poet's name and the profession of faith, the *je* of the poem assimilates a second identity. Villon, who has momentarily effaced his presence, allowing his mother to recite her soliloquy, now steps forward to join her in the culmination of her prayer.

The most obvious effect of the acrostic is to elicit multiple readings. By their vertical arrangement on the page, the letters dissociate themselves from the linear progression of the stanza and seem to fall within another plane of interpretation. At the same time they fuse the name, whether that of the poet or another individual, into the text and require the reader to interpret the organic connection. In a sense, the acrostic subverts the normative reading process. Villon is again teaching the reader how to read the poem, by demonstrating that a "conventional" reading may only reveal partial meaning of a text.

5

the "Belle Leçon"

The lengthiest section of the *Testament* in which Villon addresses his reader is the passage Marot entitled "Belle leçon aux enfants perdus." The *leçon,* comprised of sixty verses (1668–1727) including the "Ballade de bonne doctrine," normally appears in quotation marks, an editorial insertion intended to delineate the *leçon* from its immediate context. For reasons cited earlier, I believe that this passage is directly addressed to the intended readers, whom Villon variously designates as *beaulx enfans* (1668), *mes clercs* (1670), and *compains de galle* (1720). Given the length of the passage, its obvious orientation toward a very specific group of readers, and the didactic character that sets it apart from much of the *Testament,* the "Belle leçon aux enfants perdus" clearly merits separate treatment in my study. If one accepts the hypothesis that the audience addressed in the "lesson" is in fact the same audience to which the entire poem is addressed, then the centrality of this passage is inescapable. Even if this assumption is not accepted, the passage is one that invites attention and reflection. Although Villon often communicates with his reader through various types of "coded" messages— closed images, equivocal statements, ironic overtones, antiphrasis—the straightforward presentation and relatively transparent language of the *leçon* make its message more accessible.

The "Belle leçon" is introduced by a brief preliminary, commenting that it is intended for the "lost children" who may be found with Marion l'Idole. (The prostitutes Marion l'Idole and

Jeanne de Bretagne have just been named recipients of the right to "tenir publicque escole / Ou l'escollier le maistre enseigne" [1630–1631: "I give the running of that public school / Where the pupil drills the teacher"]). Villon then prefaces the lesson with an exhortation to his pupils:

> Une leçon de mon escolle
> Leur liray, qui ne dure guerre;
> Teste n'ayent dure ne folle,
> Escoutent! car c'est la derniere. (1664–1667)

> [One lesson from my school
> I'll read them, it won't take a minute
> Since they're not pigheaded or foolish
> They'll listen, it's the last they get.]

The verb *liray* distinguishes the lesson, a written lecture to be formally delivered, from the generally spoken discourse of the *Testament* ("je *dy* voir" [181], "En riens de luy je ne *mesdiz* [20]). The assertion that this lesson will be the last of a series implies that other lessons have been discreetly introduced into the poem. This is not, in fact, the first time that a didactic element has appeared in the *Testament*. The commentary on sin and repentance early in the poem, for example, has a definite moralistic flavor:

> Combien que pechiez si soit ville,
> Riens ne het que perseverance. (103–104)

> [Even the most wretched of sinners
> God hates only his perseverance.]

The story of Alexander and Diomedes and the frequent use of proverbs also belong to the poet's repertoire of lessons. The author/professor teaches his reader/pupil not by self-righteously proposing his life as an exemplary existence but rather by directing attention to the failures with which he and others like him are painfully well acquainted. This is the *escolle* from which his lessons are drawn, the school which:

M'ouvrist plus que tous les commens
D'Averroÿs sur Arristote. (95–96)

[More than the *Commentaries*
Of Averroës opened Aristotle.]

In a sense, the entire *Testament* is a "belle leçon" drawn on a vast
source of experiential knowledge and wisdom.

The didactic element is reinforced by the testamentary
framework of the poem. Although conventional examples of the
satirical testament bear little resemblance to the actual medieval
will, the *Testament* is patterned much more closely on the legal
prototype.[1] Villon's first poetic will, by contrast, is much more
closely aligned to the traditional satiric will. The *Lais* is comprised almost entirely of farcical bequests loosely ordered in the
form of a will. The character of the will, however, never develops
beyond the conventional outlines dictated by the genre. Aside
from serving as both a vehicle for humor and a structural device
intended to give the poem some semblance of order, the form of
the will fulfills no important function. The case of the *Testament*
is more complex. One of the most important features of the *Testament,* separating it from the *Lais* and earlier satiric wills, is its
emphasis on death. Whether in the awareness of mortality evident in the opening verse, the graphic description of the *agoni-
sant,* variations on the *ubi sunt* theme, the contemplation of
dismembered skeletons in the Cemetery of the Innocents, the
requiem prayer and the epitaph the poet composes for himself,
or the seemingly flippant funeral oration of the closing ballade,
the *Testament* never escapes the shadow of death. Thus, Villon
restores to the will its original spiritual dimension.[2] As one ex-
pert on fifteenth-century French wills points out, these documents represent more than mere secular concerns:

Les invocations pieuses si universelles et si développées qu'ils contien-
nent nous permettent de conclure, sans pouvoir être taxé d'exagération,
qu'au point de vue purement formaliste, le testament du xvᵉ siècle est
un acte religieux.[3]

[The pious invocations, so universal and so well developed, that they contain allow us to conclude, without being accused of exaggeration, that from a purely formalistic point of view, the will of the fifteenth century is a religious act.]

The didactic thrust of the "Belle leçon" is also strengthened by the deathbed from which the will is dictated. For the medieval mind, the deathbed was the center of not only a visible human drama but also an invisible spiritual drama of far greater significance. The visible actors would include the dying man or woman, at least one priest administering the last sacraments, those persons caring for the patient's physical needs, possibly a clerk hurriedly recording the last will and testament, members of the immediate family waiting helplessly or impatiently for the end to come. The invisible actors, graphically depicted in numerous drawings of the late medieval period, would include various angels and demons vying for the soul of the dying person.[4] At this intensely dramatic moment the eternal fate of a human existence hangs precariously between salvation and perdition. Philippe Ariès describes the situation of a medieval man confronting imminent death:

L'alternative du mourant médiéval était la suivante: ou bien ne pas cesser de jouir des *temporalia,* hommes et choses, et perdre son âme, comme lui disaient les hommes d'Eglise et toute la tradition chrétienne, ou bien y renoncer et gagner son salut éternel: *temporalia aut aeterna?*[5]

[The choice of the medieval individual facing death was the following: either not cease enjoying the *temporalia,* men and things, and lose his soul, as the men of the Church and all of Christian tradition told him, or else renounce it and attain eternal salvation: *temporalia aut aeterna?*]

Precisely within this spiritual context Villon situates the whole of the *Testament.* Thus, the "Belle leçon" functions at two levels. As the lecture of Professor Villon, it exhorts the *beaux enfants* to reexamine their values and to weigh the hope of material gain against the threat of spiritual loss. As the meditation of a dying testator, the *povre Villon,* it points to the ultimate choice that every individual must eventually confront, blurring the distinction between the living and the dying.

After attracting the attention of his audience and emphasizing the importance of the lecture about to be delivered, Villon begins the *leçon:*

> Beaulx enfans, vous perdez la plus
> Belle roze de vo chappeau;
> Mes clercs pres prenans comme glus,
> Se vous alez a Montpipeau
> Ou a Rüel, gardez la peau,
> Car pour s'esbatre en ces deux lieux,
> Cuidant que vaulsist le rappeau,
> Le perdyt Colin de Cayeulx. (1668–1675)

> [Sweet children you're throwing away
> The prettiest rose in your caps
> My clerks with fingers like glue
> If you go to Montpipeau
> Or Rueil watch you don't lose your skins
> From working those two places
> Believing an appeal could save him
> Colin de Cayeux lost his.]

The word *peau* occurs in some form four times in the stanza—prefigured in the last syllable of *chappeau* and *Montpipeau,* echoed in *rappeau*—and the phrase "gardez la peau" thus reverberates a repeated warning at regular intervals. The phrase, strategically situated in the middle of the *huitain,* occupies, structurally and thematically, a central position in the stanza. It forms a connective link between "la plus belle roze," life in full bloom, and the memory of Colin de Cayeux, a man who did not succeed in saving his skin. Colin is mentioned at two other points in Villon's poetry, once in an equivocal reference (*Testament,* verse 861: *cayeux* ostensibly meaning "notebooks," but also designating Colin's family name), and again in the opening stanza of a ballade written in jargon, a passage that, despite its "underground" language, bears a remarkable resemblance to the stanza quoted above:

Coquillars en aruans a ruel
Men ys vous chante que gardés
Que n'y laissez et corps et pel
Qu'on fist de Collin l'escallier
Devant la roe babiller
Il babigna pour son salut
Pas ne sçavoit oingnons peller
Dont l'amboureux luy rompt le suc.[6]

(Coquillards qui travaillez dans la dégringolade, moi je vous dis que vous preniez garde à ne pas y laisser le corps et la peau et que l'on a fait Colin de Cayeux parler devant la justice; il débita des bobards pour sauver sa vie, mais il ne savait pas raconter des histoires. Pour finir, le bourreau lui rompit la nuque.)

[Coquillards, you who are headed for a fall, I tell you to watch out not to leave behind your skin and body, and [tell you] that they made Colin de Cayeux speak before the judge; he told some tall stories to save his life, but he didn't know how to tell them right. In the end, the hangman broke his neck.]

The general similarity between the two quotations—each of which contains the word *ruel,* a term belonging to the jargon of the *Coquillards*—suggests that both passages may be directed to the same audience. Although the possibility of an affiliation between the primary audience of the *Testament* and the *Coquillards* does exist, evidence of this connection, or even of Villon's own connection with the *Coquillards,* is too tenuous to sustain any conclusion beyond simple conjecture. The "Belle leçon" does make it clear, however, that those whom it warns are not unacquainted with criminal activities.

The reference to Colin de Cayeux immediately personalizes the *leçon,* offering the reader a concrete example, drawn from his own milieu, of the possible consequence of a criminal life, namely a criminal death. It is known that Colin de Cayeux had been approximately the same age as Villon, also from the quarter of Saint-Benoît-le-Bétourné, and it has been suggested that the two were boyhood friends.[7] The son of a locksmith, Colin became adept at picking locks and used his skills in the theft of Navarre and other burglaries. Eventually apprehended and charged with a series of larcenies, he tried unsuccessfully to have his case transferred to ecclesiastical jurisdiction because of his clerical status and was hanged in 1460. Thus, the reference to Colin's execution forcefully drives home the lesson, evoking a familiar ghost. The intended reader, who in all probability had known Colin de Cayeux as more than a casual acquaintance and had possibly even witnessed his public execution, here confronts a victim with whom he can easily identify.

The modified form of the possessive adjective that occurs in the second verse of the stanza—*vo*—is a Picard form, which according to Jean Dufournet may be a deliberate reminder of Colin's Picard origins.[8] This interpretation opens the possibility that among its other timbres, the voice reciting the lesson carries a haunting resonance belonging to the recently deceased Colin, speaking of himself in the third person as Villon occasionally does. Exploiting the reader's aural or visual memory of Colin de Cayeux, Villon recasts the *ubi sunt* of the earlier ballade trilogy into a form that brings the reader into far more immediate contact with death.

The image of the strangled Colin de Cayeux hangs over the rest of the *leçon,* setting a tone of grim reflection that undercuts any potential for humor. Although ironic overtones are always possible in passages where the poet speaks of himself, it is difficult to imagine how a reference to the fate of the unfortunate Colin, in the absence of any clues pointing to possible ambiguity, could signal humor. Rather than drawing on the gallows as a source of black humor, Villon moves directly from physical dangers to spiritual consequences:

> Ce n'est pas ung jeu de troys mailles,
> Ou va corps, et peult estre l'ame.
> Qui pert, riens n'y font repentailles
> C'on n'en meurre a honte et diffame,
> Et qui gaigne n'a pas a femme

Dido, la royne de Cartaige.
L'omme est donc bien fol et infame
Qui pour si peu couche tel gaige. (1676–1683)

[There's no three-penny game
Where the body's at stake and perhaps the soul
If you lose repenting won't save you
From dying in shame and disgrace
And if you win you won't get to marry
Dido the queen of Carthage
The man's despicable and a fool
Who wagers so much for so little.]

The stanza is semantically polarized between material and spiritual values: *jeu, corps, pert,* and *gaigne* playing against *ame, repentailles, meurre.* The semantic struggle for domination parallels the conflict between secular and religious concerns at the core of the "Belle leçon." While the secular element appears to achieve lexical domination in the last word of the stanza, the term *gaige* is invested with spiritual significance, referring to the real stakes of the dangerous game, that is, the eternal fate of the soul. The same choice will be similarly expressed two centuries later in Pascal's famous passage on the *pari:*

—Oui, mais il faut parier. Cela n'est pas volontaire, vous êtes embarqué. Lequel prendrez-vous donc? Voyons, puisqu'il faut choisir, voyons ce qui vous intéresse le moins.[9]

[—Yes, but you have to gamble. It's not voluntary; you have no choice. Which will you take then? Well, since you have to choose, let's see what is to your least advantage.]

Like Pascal's attempt at persuasion, Villon's argument has the compelling force of a logical demonstration. The *donc* of the penultimate verse lends a syllogistic authority to the conclusion of the stanza, as the *leçon* progresses in good scholastic fashion.

From deductive logic the speaker moves to folk wisdom, seeking additional sources to support his thesis. Reworking a

proverbial phrase, he reminds his listeners that material wealth
is quickly consumed:

> On dit, et il est verité,
> Que charecterie se boit toute,
> Au feu l'iver, au boys l'esté. (1685–1687)

> [There's a saying and it's true
> The winecart driver drinks all his load
> Winter by the fire, summer in the woods.]

This reflection leads into the "Ballade de bonne doctrine" (1692–
1719) in which the life of the listeners is presented as a cycle of
crime and squandering whose only objective is repeated gratification of the senses:

> Ou en va l'acquest que cuidez?
> Tout aux tavernes et aux filles. (1698–1699)

> [Where does the loot go, do you think?
> All to the taverns and girls.]

The *leçon* concludes with a direct address in which the audience
is forcefully urged to consider the gravity of a choice that cannot
be escaped:

> A vous parle, compains de galle,
> Mal des ames et bien du corps:
> Gardez vous tous de ce mau halle
> Qui noircist les gens quant sont mors;
> Eschevez le, c'est ung mal mors.
> Passez vous au mieulx que pourrez,
> Et, pour Dieu, soiez tous recors:
> Une foyz viendra que mourrez. (1720–1727)

> [I mean you, comrades in revels
> Healthy in body but sick in soul
> Watch out all of you for that dry rot
> That turns men black when they're dead

93

Stand back, it has a bad bite
Just get by as best you can
And, for the love of God, remember
A time will come when you'll die.]

The *mau halle* of the third verse may either be applied to *corps* or
ames in the preceding verse. In one sense, Villon is evoking the
sight of exposed, blackened corpses, like those given voice in the
"Epitaphe Villon," left hanging from the gallows for public edification. But the image also warns of an even graver consequence,
the *mau halle* being the infernal heat that awaits the unrepentant
sinner.

Upon reflection, it can be seen that the "Belle leçon aux
enfants perdus" follows a logically structured progression involving several distinct divisions. The lesson opens with a warning
of the physical risks involved in a life of crime and forcefully
illustrates this point by evoking the fate of Colin de Cayeux
(1668–1675). A consideration of physical danger is succeeded
by reflection on the spiritual "stakes" at risk (1676–1683). The
reader/listener is, for the moment, distanced from the drama by
the use of impersonal terms: *qui, on, l'omme.* The next section
(1684–1719) represents an extended illustration of the futility of
material gain, expanding on the *si peu* of "Qui pour si peu couche
tel gaige" (1683). In the last section of the lesson (1720–1727)
the moral is drawn and directly applied to the audience without
the protective mediation of impersonal terms. The lesson ends,
as it began, in the shadow of the gallows, and it becomes clear
that "la plus belle roze de vo chappeau" is more than just physical
well-being. The final two verses of the "Belle leçon" point to a
judgment that transcends the human justice of the hangman's
scaffold.

All the lesson's grim warnings, taken with its relative lack
of discernible ambiguity, argue in favor of a genuine didactic
intention. Of all the conflicts to be found in the *Testament,* perhaps the most prevalent and most fundamental is the tug of war
between good and evil. Throughout the poem we witness a con-

stantly renewed struggle between these two elemental forces. Moments of spiritual illumination occur sporadically but repeatedly. The figure of the resurrected Christ evoked early in the poem (99–100), the "Ballade pour prier Notre Dame," various references to the Last Judgment, and veiled allusions to the Crucifixion contained in the final ballade, all represent an element of hope and redemption. This salvific force, however, is constantly threatened by sinful intentions. Moments of illumination are separated by long stretches of spiritual darkness during which Villon descends to the depths of the psyche, reminding us of the human capacity for malice, cruelty, violence, and despair. It often seems the demons outnumber if not outmatch the angels.

Given this moral tension underlying the entire *Testament*, a tension intensified by the testamentary framework and the fiction of the deathbed, it is not surprising that the longest passage addressed directly to the reader is definitely didactic.[10] According to Pierre-Yves Badel, a primary motive evident in the *Testament* is the desire to instruct:

> Villon a choisi d'écrire dans une forme qui n'est pas celle des poètes lyriques, mais celle de longs traités didactiques comme le *Champion des dames* de Martin le Franc. Son intention n'est pas de se chanter ou de se plaindre, mais d'abord comme celle de Bodel, Rutebeuf et Jean de Meun, d'enseigner.[11]

> [Villon chose to write in the form which is not that of the lyric poets, but that of long didactic treatises like *Champion des dames* of Martin le Franc. His intention is not to sing or complain about himself, but first of all, like Bodel, Rutebeuf, and Jean de Meun, to instruct.]

The ramifications of Badel's remarks are relevant to my study; I will return to these implications.

The "Belle leçon" fulfills a number of important roles in the *Testament*. First, despite the postponement of its appearance until relatively late in the poem, it serves a certain dedicatory function, collectively naming the readers, claiming to be written for their edification, and implying that the entire poem may be taken as an extension of this little lesson. Second, it reestablishes the authority of the speaker's discourse, subject to repeated attack. Whether answering specific charges or anticipating possible questions and objections, the author is constantly allowing the reader (or *a* reader) to interrupt his train of thought. The accumulated effect of these repeated disruptions challenges the authority of the narrative voice. Each response to a question or attack underlines a vulnerability to external interference. By the same token, each response strengthens the protesting voices, increasing their power to shape the discourse of the poem with their doubts and queries. By constantly attempting to legitimize itself, the narrative voice establishes a defensive posture without ever successfully disarming the opposition. In the "Belle leçon" the author manages, if only provisionally, to reassert his authority. This authority belongs to not only the lectern but also the pulpit, for the *leçon* becomes a sermon as well as a lecture; the onus of sin is now transferred from the author to the reader.

The "Belle leçon" derives much of its power from the fact that it is not a harangue against crime, given for the benefit of an anonymous public, but an admonition sharply focused on a specific audience whose acquaintance with crime is more than superficial, a group that Gert Pinkernell characterizes as "jeunes intellectuels . . . appartenant à un monde marginalisé, honni et persécuté, plein de rudesses, voire de brutalité" ["young intellectuals . . . belonging to a marginalized world, a shamed and persecuted world, full of roughness, even brutality"].[12] The various crimes detailed in the "Ballade de bonne doctrine" do not represent hypothetical possibilities but rather, in all likelihood, activities in which some of the original readers had actually been engaged. Nor is the sad example of Colin de Cayeux taken from imaginary sources; it is from the very group to which the *leçon* is directed. In short, the lesson "hits home," and it hits hard.

Unless the passage is taken as a simple parody, totally devoid of serious intent—a reading that, as I have attempted to demonstrate, cannot be supported by internal evidence—the "Belle leçon" is compelling proof that the author's relationship with his reader is not neutral. The attitude underlying the playful jibes, shared innuendos, gentle teasing, and coarse jokes, all of which unite the author with his reader, becomes explicit in the "Belle leçon." The attitude, in simplest terms, is one of affection. Indeed, given the intimate relationship between the author and his entourage, it is hardly possible that the literary relationship could be based on neutrality. The author/reader position, insofar as it reflects an actual social relationship, is based on solidarity, shared values, and mutual support. The work is grounded on a premise of reciprocal respect and sympathy, which, to borrow a term recently in vogue, is sometimes called "male bonding." The *Testament* is not only a man's poem but also a poem for particular men, individuals united by their marginal position in a society from which they find themselves largely excluded. In this context, the warning to "mes clercs" takes on an element of moral responsibility. Whatever else the *leçon* may be and however one chooses to interpret its tone, the passage addresses the ultimate physical, moral, and spiritual dangers confronting Villon and his readers; and thus it speaks to the core of their condition, to the commonalities that unite them at the deepest level.

The presence of didacticism in no way detracts from the satiric and ironic aspects of the *Testament,* which remain its salient stylistic features. Still one should not assume that humor is necessarily incompatible with moral concerns. In fact, many works included in the canon of late medieval classics represent a skillful blend of comic and didactic intent—*The Canterbury Tales, The Decameron, The Celestina,* to cite a few of the most prominent titles. Early in the *Testament,* in the story of Alexander and Diomedes, Villon already shows evidence of a strong didactic hand. Vladimir Rossman comments on the moral implications of the anecdote:

> The story of Alexander and Diomedes is an illustration of the relationship between God and Villon the sinner. The change of fortune "mauvaise en bonne" (1. 156) in the pagan story corresponds to the sinner's

repentancé—i.e., to his transition from sin and damnation to mercy. . . . In any case, as repentance brings Villon closer to God, so reversal of fortune brings Diomedes closer in status to Alexander. [13]

It is virtually impossible to find a major work of French literature written in the late medieval period that does not incorporate an important didactic element. Thus, the relationship between Villon and his reader around which the poem is largely shaped can hardly be expected to be free of didactic coloring. Villon clearly wishes to draw the reader's attention to the insubstantiality of social values and the inherent limitations of human justice. But overarching these issues lies the more basic and far more important problem of good and evil. The battle fought over the deathbed of the *Testament,* the momentous struggle in which the "Belle leçon" urges its listeners to engage, the conflict between the light of hope and the darkness of despair that unfolds within the poem, all mirror and intensify the spiritual battle that Villon and his readers, as medieval Christians, are forced to fight at every moment. In this sense, the *Testament* unmistakably bears a religious imprint: it is at once a deeply personal and a deeply medieval work.

6

the two readers

Not all of Villon's poetry is directed to a particular, highly restricted audience. Thus far, my study has focused mainly on the intended reader and his expected role in the "performance" of Villon's poetry. There is, however, another reader for whom Villon writes, a reader who is not expected to bring any privileged knowledge to his reading of a given text. For purposes of convenience, this second type of reader may be labeled the "anonymous reader" in contrast with the "privileged reader" whose participation in the *Testament* I have discussed at length.

Although the anonymous reader sometimes overlaps the privileged reader, as in certain passages of the *Testament* discussed in Chapter 4, it is often possible to distinguish clearly between the two. The *Lais* and the body of the *Testament,* excluding most of the ballades, are primarily directed toward the privileged reader. The majority of the ballades in the *Testament* and most of the other miscellaneous poems (which Rychner calls "les poèmes variés") are written for the anonymous reader.[1] The general criterion that makes it possible to classify Villon's poetry into these two broad categories is the degree of focus discernible within a given text. The passages directed to the privileged reader are sharply focused on the reader, in the sense that they rely on him to flesh out images, interpret tones, discern ironic meanings, supply pertinent information, decode hidden messages, and continually read the text against his personal knowledge of the author. The passages directed to the anonymous reader (or, perhaps more accurately stated, the undirected passages) are those whose comprehension does not require highly specific knowledge on the part of a particular reader.

As I have indicated, my primary objective is to examine the role of Villon's privileged reader. For the purpose of comparison, however, I would like to briefly consider a representative example of Villon's "undirected" poetry. The following excerpt, the opening of the famous "Ballade des pendus" (or "L'Epitaphe Villon"), illustrates Villon's adeptness at drawing the reader—any reader—into the text:

> Freres humains qui aprés nous vivez,
> N'ayez les cueurs contre nous endurcis,
> Car se pitié de nous povres avez,
> Dieu en aura plus tost de vous mercis.
> Vous nous voiez cy attachez, cinq, six:
> Quant de la chair que trop avons nourrie,
> El est pieça devoree et pourrie,
> Et nous, les os, devenons cendre et pouldre.
> De nostre mal personne ne s'en rie,
> Mais priez Dieu que tous nous vueille absouldre. (1–10)

> [Brother humans who live on after us
> Don't let your hearts harden against us
> For if you have pity on wretches like us
> More likely God will show mercy to you
> You see us five, six, hanging here
> As for the flesh we loved too well
> A while ago it was eaten and has rotted away
> And we the bones turn to ashes and dust
> Let no one make us the butt of jokes
> But pray God that he absolve us all.]

The opening verse immediately establishes a rapport between the voice, whether solo or choral, and those whom it addresses.

At one level, the voice is clearly directed to the witnesses for whose benefit the bodies have been left suspended from the gallows. At another level, the *freres humains* encompass all the living, each successive generation of humanity "qui aprés nous vivez." The ambiguity of the phrase turns on *aprés,* which may be taken in a restricted sense (immediately after) or in a broader sense (henceforth). The space separating the voice from the listener is not time but death. Time, in fact, does not exist in the ballade. The voice, unrestricted by temporal limits, speaks from the realm of eternity, addressing all those who eventually pass within its hearing. The word from the gallows, then, reaches across death toward the living, all of whom are within its range. Thus, the reader relates to the voice not only through the intermediary of a fifteenth-century observer with whom he may identify but also as the direct recipient of the hanged men's urgent pleas.

Also present in the opening verse is an opposition that will generate the main dramatic tension in the ballade, namely the conflict between alienation and affinity. On one hand, the chasm separating the speaker from the listener is immediately apparent; on the other hand, the familiar form of address suggests a certain proximity, a common destiny. The opposition is concentrated in *vivez;* this word stresses the fundamental distinction separating the two realms of existence while simultaneously reminding the reader of the bond of mortality that links him to the figures hanging over the scaffold.

The second verse confers a double advantage on the listener/reader. Not only is he alive and thus capable of avoiding the errors that led the victims to their unenviable fate, but also, by the very fact that he is able to witness the visible results of these errors, he finds himself in a morally superior position. Thus, the *vous* is alienated from the *nous* both metaphysically and morally. The figurative use of *endurcis* parallels the rigidity of the exposed corpses, implying that both flesh and hearts are equally susceptible to hardening. The next two verses implicitly invoke the Biblical injunction against judgment: "Pass no judgment, and you will not be judged; do not condemn, and you will not be condemned."[2] The *mercis* promised to the living is conditional upon forgiving the sins of the dead. Thus, the salvation of the *vous* is inextricably bound with the sins of the *nous*. The illusion of moral superiority dissolves as human justice is framed within the larger context of divine justice. As the boundary between life and death is only a temporary barrier separating the dead from the survivors, so the boundary of human justice separating the innocent from the condemned is only a temporary barrier that will become meaningless when superseded by the Last Judgment.

As the voice proceeds to describe the scene from which it emanates, the ambiguity of the *vous* is reinforced. Ostensibly, the voice simply verbalizes the image that the viewer is presently contemplating. The redundancy of this verbalization, however, militates against restricting the description to such a facile interpretation. Although it is not invalid to read the series of images as the translation of a visually present scene into poetic language, it is equally plausible to take the description as a reconstruction of the scene for those included among the amorphous *vous* who, deprived of direct visual access, must rely on verbal representation. This construction would explain the ballade's emphasis on vivid imagery, extending the signification of *voiez* (v. 5) beyond its literal meaning; thus, the act of seeing becomes inseparable from the act of creating. "Vous nous voiez . . ." reproduces for the viewer what he already sees and recreates for the nonviewer, the reader, what he cannot actually see. In one case, the phrase is flatly factual; in the other, it becomes powerfully evocative. The verse seems to play with creative potential as the first broad lines of the scene are sketched in: "Vous nous voiez cy attachez, cinq, six." To be sure, one may choose to prosaically interpret the numbers as the conclusion of an enumeration, but the verse need not be read in so pedestrian a fashion. The numerical imprecision may also reflect a natural hesitancy in the creative process, as the vision is followed immediately by a revision. The "correction" of the original number, while pointless if directed to a visual observer, reminds the reader that, although the details of the scene are imaginary and thus subject to modification, the essence of the ballade is based not on its specificity but on the illusion of communication between the *nous* and the *vous,* the *pendus* and the reader.

The next three verses, describing the gruesome appearance of the decayed corpses, broadly outline the transformation that these once healthy bodies have undergone. Literally and figuratively freed of the burden of flesh, the condemned have been stripped of all carnal concerns. The image of human cadavers reduced to skeletal remains, likely to inspire more revulsion than sympathy, apparently reinforce the reader's sense of alienation. But grotesque though the remains may be, they graphically represent the frailty of the human body, and, having lost the flesh that guaranteed them each a distinctive identity, they bear witness to a common human destiny. Like the figures of the *danse macabre,* the dancing skeletons of the ballade

> Jamais nul temps nous ne sommes assis
> Puis ça, puis la, comme le vent varie (25–26)
>
> [Never ever can we stand still
> Now here, now there, as the wind shifts]

represent the ultimate fate of all human conditions. Thus, the *vous,* the witness, the reader is forced to contemplate an image that at the most profound level is an image of himself. Like a macabre mirror, the hanging figures reflect a ghastly transformation of the living viewer. But instead of showing him a distorted image, an illusion from which he can safely distance himself, the figures reflect the very essence of the viewer's physical reality; the skeleton is the universal medieval symbol of mortality. Thus, the reader, confronting the reflection of his own essential nature in the grim figures suspended from the gallows, is forced into the realization that the boundary separating him from the executed criminals is merely an illusion.

The *nous* that identifies itself in the eighth verse as "*les os,*" represents not just the physical remains of the dead but also their souls, and the spiritual rather than the corporal entity voices the moving plea for salvation in the *envoi:*

> Prince Jhesus qui sur tous a maistrie,
> Garde qu'Enfer n'ait de nous seigneurie:
> A luy n'ayons que faire ne que souldre! (31–33)

> [Prince Jesus, master over all
> Don't let us fall into hell's dominion
> We've nothing to do or settle down there.]

As the salvation of the living is entwined with the sins of the dead, likewise the salvation of the dead is dependent on the prayers of the living: "Mais priez Dieu que tous nous vueille absouldre." The *tous nous* of the refrain, however, is not limited to the five or six souls that stand in immediate need of absolution but extends to include the reader, and even all of humanity. Having dispelled the illusion of "otherness," showing the reader that his own fate cannot be separated from that of his *frères humains,* the poem dissolves the barrier between the living and the dead, between the innocent and the guilty. The opposition between the *vous* and the *nous* ultimately disappears, merging into the all-embracing *tous nous.*

The dynamics of reader response obviously vary according to the specific reader whom Villon engages in his text. In general, the poetry directed to the privileged reader manifests an abundance of autobiographical allusions, a fluctuation of tone, and an adept manipulation of equivocal language for humorous effect. By contrast, the language of the poetry directed to the anonymous reader tends to be less localized, more rhetorical, and more transparent. Thus, each orientation evokes a different range of reader responses. The poetry written for the *compains de galle* conveys a quality of immediacy, closely connected to the historical moment of its creation. The rest of Villon's verse, the portion of his work largely responsible for his "canonization" among the elect of French letters, possesses a depth, a universality that has opened and endeared it to posterity.

The dual orientation of the *Testament,* alternating between the privileged and the anonymous reader, supports the theory advanced by Siciliano (and accepted by LeGentil and others) that the work assembles numerous shorter lyric pieces written at various dates prior to the composition of the *Testament.*[3] In selecting certain ballades for inclusion in his long poetic will, Villon created what LeGentil calls "sa propre anthologie."[4] Although portions of Villon's magnum opus may well have been written with an eye to posterity, one immediate motive for its composition was, in all probability, to provide his friends with an anthology of his poetry. Many modern readers undoubtedly consider the ballades artistically superior to the rest of the work, which they regard as filling material of lesser quality. I can only conjecture to what degree this perception may have been shared by the author and his original readers. For the purposes of the present study, the fact that two reader orientations exist in the *Testament* is more important than attempting to establish relative aesthetic merit.

Although the sixteen ballades incorporated into the *Testament* represent a wide spectrum of thematic and stylistic variation, one should not assume that they are forcibly and randomly inserted into the poem. On the contrary, they are generally integrated into the poetic will with consummate artistry. In a separate study I have examined the antithetical symmetry connecting two seemingly unrelated and randomly juxtaposed ballades— "Ballade pour Robert d'Estouteville" and "Ballade des langues ennuyeuses."[5] Still, the contrast between the "open" and the "closed" passages remains readily apparent, and the continual fluctuation between the two contributes greatly to the poem's complexity and elasticity. If the *Testament* were a musical piece, these contrasting orientations might take the form of two different keys alternately dominating the composition. Only at the very end of the work do the two keys finally merge in a moment of harmonious resolution. The piece that concludes the series of ballades and also the *Testament* itself relates the death of the *povre Villon:*

Icy se clost le testament
Et finist du povre Villon.
Venez a son enterrement,
Quant vous orez le carillon,
Vestuz rouge com vermeillon,
Car en amours mourut martir;
Ce jura il sur son coullon,
Quant de ce monde voult partir.

Et je croy bien que pas n'en ment,
Car chassié fut comme ung soullon
De ses amours, hayneusement,
Tant que d'icy a Roussillon
Brosses n'y a ne brossillon
Qui n'eust, ce dit il sans mentir,
Ung lambeau de son cotillon,
Quant de ce monde voult partir.

Il est ainsi et tellement:
Quant mourut, n'avoit q'un haillon;
Qui plus, en mourant, mallement
L'espoignoit d'Amours l'esguillon;
Plus agu que le ranguillon
D'un baudrier lui faisoit sentir
—C'est de quoy nous esmerveillon—,
Quant de ce monde voult partir.

Prince gent comme esmerillon,
Saichiez qu'il fist au departir;
Ung traict but de vin morillon,
Quant de ce monde voult partir. (1996–2023)

[Here ends and finishes
The testament of poor Villon
Come to his burial
When you hear the bell ringing
Dressed in red vermillion
For he died a martyr to love
This he swore on his testicle
As he made his way out of this world.

And I think it wasn't a lie
For he was chased like a scullion

By his loves so spitefully
From here to Roussillon
There isn't a bush or a shrub
That didn't get, he speaks truly
A shred from his back
As he made his way out of this world.

It was like this, so that
By the time he died he had only a rag
What's worse, as he died, sorely
The spur of love pricked into him
Sharper than the buckle-tongue
Of a baldric he could feel it
And this is what we marvel at
As he made his way out of this world.

Prince graceful as a merlin
Hear what he did as he left
He took a long swig of dead-black wine
As he made his way out of this world.]

The intratextual reference of the first two verses strongly suggests that the composition of the ballade is contemporary with the writing of the *Testament*. At any rate, the verses firmly and logically situate the piece in relation to the longer poem that it concludes. The voice of the dying testator has now been replaced by an unidentified voice eulogizing the deceased. In one sense, the ballade bears a certain affinity to other "closed" passages of the work. The protagonist whose death is related here shares with the poet more than just a name, and the privileged reader, once finding Villon's name in the second verse, will inevitably filter the fiction of the ballade through his knowledge of its creator. The characterization of the deceased as a man repeatedly victimized by love corresponds to a series of cryptic comments in the *Testament,* all of which relate directly or indirectly to certain personal experiences undoubtedly known to Villon's immediate audience.[6]

The final ballade obviously contains a core of truth, without which it would drift meaninglessly detached from the rest of the work. On the other hand, to interpret the ballade as the accurate representation of a bitter disillusionment with love deprives the piece of possible ironic overtones suggested by the repeated insistence on veracity: "Ce jura il sur son coullon" (2002), "Et je croy bien que pas n'en ment" (2004), and "ce dit il sans mentir" (2009). The humorous thrust of the ballade is clearly based on a combination of truth and exaggeration. Where one ends and the other begins, we, unlike the privileged reader, cannot possibly determine.

While the ballade addresses the privileged reader at one level, it addresses all other readers at another. With its strong epitaphic character, the ballade is actually an expansion of the epitaph (1884–1903). A phrase from the epitaph ("Qu'Amours occist de son raillon" ["One love's arrow struck down"; 1885]) is even reworked in the ballade ("Qui plus en mourant, mallement / L'espoignoit d'Amours l'esguillon [2014–2015]), making explicit the connective link between the two passages. As an epitaph the ballade fixes the memory of the deceased for all posterity, selectively including those aspects of his life that are to be remembered, discreetly omitting those to be forgotten. Like the inscription on a grave, the ballade speaks anonymously and indiscriminately to all who read it.

The two types of readers, given their different perspectives, will create two distinct readings of the same text. One reader will see in the *povre Villon* the caricature of a man with whom he is well acquainted. The various references to banishment, destitution, physical abuse, and sexual adventures and misadventures will be seen as corresponding to known biographical circumstances, a correspondence that enriches the ballade with personal significance while heightening the comic effect of its farcical distortion.

The other reader, perhaps sensing the biographical basis of the poem, will inevitably connect the *povre Villon* to the *je* of the *Testament,* relating the account of the mock martyr's life and death to familiar thematic patterns they appear to parallel. In short, where one reader will recognize in the text the image of a man, the other reader will recognize in the text the image of another text. The second reading, while possibly less rich than the first, has nonetheless a certain validity. For if the *povre Villon* is indissociably connected to the historical Villon, he adheres with equal strength to the narrative voice by which we know Villon. At the same time that he plays to his private "claque," Villon appears conscious of a wider audience. Speaking of himself in the third person and the past tense, he transcends his own mortality, adopting the stance of a detached observer attempting to make sense of the life of the *povre Villon;* his stance bears a remarkable resemblance to that of the anonymous reader. Highlighting salient thematic features of the *Testament,* the *je* of the ballade interprets not only the life of the protagonist but also the poem itself. Thus, Villon, in effect, joins the ranks of all his readers, numbering himself among them in another all-inclusive *nous:* "C'est de quoy nous esmerveillon" (2018).

As the *envoi* of the earliest ballades was written to formally dispatch the poem to its destination, so this ballade, the *envoi* of the *Testament,* simultaneously dispatches the *povre Villon* and the *Testament* on their respective journeys. The *monde* of the final verse—"Quant de ce monde voult partir"—is the world of the *Testament* as well as the *ici-bas,* and the departure of the protagonist thus coincides with the reader's departure from the text. It is significant that both the last and first acts of the *Testament* involve drinking—the last in a literal sense, the first in a figurative sense:

> En l'an de mon trentiesme aage,
> Que toutes mes hontes j'euz beues. (1–2)
>
> [In the thirtieth year of life
> When I had drunk down all my disgrace.]

Is the parallel coincidental, or could the final drink, among other possible meanings, be an invitation to the reader to give the poem another reading?

7

another poet,
another audience

François Villon is not the only late medieval poet whose work reflects an influential awareness of a specific audience. However, a thorough examination of reader-response patterns in fifteenth-century French poetry would far exceed the scope of the present study. Furthermore, this aspect of medieval poetics is so complex that a broad overview would only present, at best, a superficial, vastly simplified assessment, which would contribute very little toward the appreciation of Villon's distinctive rapport with his audience. Rather than attempt a synoptic characterization applying to all poetry of the period, I prefer, in the interests of concision and clarity of focus, to limit myself to a single poet. The purpose of this chapter is not to illustrate a poetic norm against which Villon's originality detaches itself but rather to show how "private poetry" of the period easily lends itself to a variety of interactions between author and reader.

The poetry of Charles d'Orléans offers a number of convenient parallels with the poetry of Villon. The work of the *doulx seigneur,* as Villon refers to him in the "Louange à Marie d'Orléans" (v. 19), is roughly contemporaneous with the poetry of the *povre escolier* (v. 132). Like the bulk of Villon's work, most of Charles's ballades were composed for a highly restricted audience. From internal evidence it is obvious that many of the duke's ballades, serving the function of poetic correspondence, were intended for a specific recipient. As in the case of Villon's poetry, Charles d'Orléans's verse frequently attests a clear awareness of the reader's presence, an awareness expressed by a variety of explicit or implicit acknowledgments. In both cases the relationship between poet and reader remains dynamic and supple. Finally, the audience is variously represented in the text itself, as the poets dramatize their interaction with the readers.

Throughout his exile in England (1415–1440), Charles maintained contact with his homeland through a steady flow of written messages. Some of these took the form of ballades. Approached as specimens of epistolary correspondence, the poems yield little autobiographical data. Still, it is clear that they were written to serve a communicative as well as a literary function. They confirm the writer's health or state of mind, occasionally convey a minimum of circumstantial information, acknowledge receipt of correspondence, and often encourage the lady (generally assumed to be his wife Bonne) to continue writing.

In one such ballade, the poet responds to a recently received missive:

> Je ne vous puis ne sçay amer,
> Ma Dame, tant que je vouldroye;
> Car escript m'avez pour m'oster
> Ennuy qui trop fort me guerroye:
> "Mon seul amy, mon bien, ma joye,
> Cellui que sur tous amer veulx,
> Je vous pry que soyez joyeux
> En esperant que brief vous voye." [1]

> [I neither know how nor am able to love you,
> My Lady, as much as I would like;
> For you have written to rid me of
> Worry which wages cruel war against me:
> "My only friend, my wealth, my joy,
> He whom I wish to love above all others,
> I beg you that you be joyful
> While waiting for me to see you soon."]

The stanza is symmetrically divided between two voices: the first represents the poet; the second represents the woman to whom the poem is addressed. The last half of the stanza either presents a verbatim transcription taken from a recently received letter-poem or a versified paraphrase of a prose statement contained in the letter. Although the degree to which the text of the letter may have been altered cannot be determined, there is no basis to doubt that these verses either reproduce or are patterned after an authentic excerpt of correspondence. While the voice of the *je*, using the negative particle and the conditional *vouldroye*, conveys a sense of helplessness, ineffectuality, and constraint, the voice of the *Dame*, by contrast, evinces an unmistakable vigor and strength of purpose, an attitude that she invites the poet to share. With the excerpt from the letter, there is a transposition of roles as the reader becomes the writer; the writer, reader.

Having conveyed in the opening verses a sense of passivity, even paralysis, the poet eventually ceases to speak at all, yielding to the *Dame*, who brings the stanza to a forceful conclusion. In the very act of writing, the woman seems to somehow assert a dominant force, for, while the first person of the ballade appears as a subject pronoun in the first two verses, it is abruptly transformed into an object pronoun following the word *escript:* "m'avez," "m'oster," "me guerroye." The grammatical dominance of the feminine voice is further strengthened by the indirect command implicit in the subjunctive clause: "Je vous pry que soyez joyeux." Thus, the reader, given an active presence in the poem, momentarily effaces the poet completely. Reproducing the content, if not the exact verbal image of her message, the poem becomes a mirror in which the reader is shown a reflection of her own presence.

With the incorporation of the excerpt from the letter, the reader is given a voice in the ballade, and she thus becomes, in a literal sense, cocreator of the poem. Although her collaborative contribution is limited, strictly speaking, to only four verses, her imagined presence may be clearly discerned as the primary creative force. Unlike those ballades of Charles d'Orléans characterized by a decidedly introspective orientation, often so self-reflexive that the poet appears to be writing only for himself, this poem is completely centered on the presence of a specific reader, the woman who is at once the source and the object of the poetic inspiration—the very raison d'être of the ballade. The poem is less an attempt to initiate fresh communication than an acknowledgment of communication received and a demonstration of its effect upon the recipient. It is hardly accidental that virtually in the precise center of the poem are found the words *vostre message* ("Que vostre message m'envoye" [12]), graphically illustrating the centrality of the message received rather than the message presently formulated in reply.

The final verse of the quotation ascribed to the woman, "En esperant que brief vous voye," becomes the refrain of the ballade. In one sense, the refrain signals the importance of the feminine voice, reinforcing the reader's collaborative role in the creation of the poem. However, in the two instances where the verse is repeated as a refrain, it is spoken by the *je* and follows as a logical conclusion to preceding statements in the stanza. The phrase, having thus become internalized, is now applied to a different object but with an identical meaning. In effect, the verse is ultimately spoken in unison, representing a fusion of desires. Poet and reader, separated in reality by formidable stretches of space and time, are allowed to reunite momentarily in the world of poetic imagination.

As we read today this ballade or similar ballades by Charles d'Orléans, we may be left with the impression that we have understood the general sense of the poem. Indeed, the fact that we even attempt to interpret such a poem betrays a belief that, in spite of its obviously private function, the piece may be productively subjected to literary analysis. Having uncovered patterns of imagery, verbal symmetry, structural unity, we may reach the illusory conclusion that we have actually grasped the essence of the poem. This conclusion is all the more easily reached in the case of Charles d'Orléans, owing to the unusual clarity and disarming simplicity of his language and the relative abundance of existing biographical information in which to loosely frame the reading of his poems. To the degree that the act of reading is an intellectual exercise, the impression of general comprehension may be partially justified. It must be recognized, however, that reading is a psychological process drawing heavily on emotional as well as intellectual responses, and the former, as Walter Slatoff observes, cannot be validly considered as secondary to the latter:

> Moreover, the very meaning of a literary work depends on emotional responses. Most works could scarcely be comprehended by a reader who lacked all human emotions. Nor are emotional responses inherently less responsible than intellectual ones. One can read as irresponsibly intellectually as emotionally, exploit a text to satisfy intellectual needs as easily as to satisfy emotional ones. To respect a text doesn't mean to read impersonally or unemotionally any more than to respect another person means holding him at arm's length.[2]

The emotional response of the reader primarily differentiates the reading of this ballade by the intended recipient from the reading effected by any subsequent reader. To return to Rosenblatt's distinction between "text" and "poem," the poem was created by Charles d'Orléans in such a way that it would be actualized in the mind of a specific reader. The text we read today results in a different actualization. Although each reader sees a different poem, all versions share one important lacuna, namely the emotional response that the ballade was designed to elicit from its intended reader.

The ballade in question offers several points of comparison with the *Testament*. In spite of obvious divergences—differences of length, tone, style, thematic content—both works are predicated on reception by an intimate audience. Given the single recipient of Charles d'Orléans's ballade, the well-defined nature of the relationship between poet and reader, and the brevity and relative simplicity of the piece, the role of the reader is more easily studied in the ballade than in the *Testament*. Nevertheless, both literary works illustrate different applications of a common creative principle. Each work, representing an act of communication with a specific audience, is written to be fully actualized only by this particular audience with which the poet maintains a privileged rapport.

Charles d'Orléans uses a variety of means to draw his privileged reader into his poetry. In an extended image he identifies his addressee with the radiance of sunlight:

> Se Dieu plaist, briefment la nuee
> De ma tristesse passera,
> Belle tresloyaument amee,
> Et le beau temps se moustrera:
> Mais savez vous quant ce sera?
> Quant le doulx souleil gracieux
> De vostre beauté entrera
> Par les fenestres de mes yeulx. (67, 1–8)

> [If it please God, the cloud
> Of my sadness will pass,
> Lovely lady, loyally loved,
> And fair weather will show itself:
> But do you know when this will be?
> When the sweet, gracious sun
> Of your beauty enters
> Through the windows of my eyes.]

Although the ballade cited earlier in this chapter represents the interaction between the *je* and the *vous* largely in terms of written communication (*escript, motz, mander, message*), the relationship is now transposed into a purely metaphorical dimension. The woman is associated with beauty and natural light, but the poet, whose heart is sleeping in "la chambre de ma pensee" (9), is associated with confinement and darkness. Again the reader is represented as a dynamic force in contrast to the passivity and helplessness exhibited by the poet. The forceful entrance (one might even say "penetration," were it not for the unfortunate Freudian connotations the word inevitably seems to carry) of sunrays into the darkened chamber of thought parallels the introduction of the reader into the ballade, itself a kind of chamber imprisoning the poet's thought. Again the reader is shown the dramatic effect of her presence upon the poet; through poetic transformation she finds herself reunited with him, dispelling his despair and liberating him from darkness.

Although the importance of the reader's emotional response may be less conspicuous in Villon's poetry, the element is one that, as Slatoff reminds us, cannot be dismissed from any serious consideration of the reading process. Emotional response, however, is problematic because it cannot be subjected to the same methodical scrutiny that may be imposed on intellectual processes. Image formation, perception of irony, identification of hidden messages, and other activities performed by Villon's reader may be isolated and analyzed as purely mental operations. But emotional response is a much more slippery area. Even in the case of Charles d'Orléans, many of whose ballades are clearly designed to evoke a strong emotional response from the intended reader, we cannot reconstruct the affective dynamics of a poem's reception without taking our interpretive operations onto dangerously thin ice. Although emotional response is not subject to rigorous analysis, it should not be ignored. That the reading of the *Testament* by its earliest audience was an emotional as well as an intellectual exercise, we may be sure. That the work was designed to and succeeded in calling forth a wide range of emotional responses—humor, joy, anger, fear, sympathy, surprise, admiration—is virtually certain. Without being able to confirm the precise emotion that a given passage probably elicited from its intended audience, we can confidently assume that the reading of the *Testament* was for its first readers an emotionally charged experience.

Much of Charles d'Orléans's poetry was addressed to more than a single reader. The rondeaux, written after his return to France in 1440, are directed to the duke's entourage and contain frequent references to various members of his domestic staff, largely comprised of well-educated young squires from wealthy families.[3] Charles encouraged these young men to try their hand at verse, and his personal manuscript includes numerous exchanges of rondeaux. In the humor, wit, and banter of these lighthearted exchanges, a spirit of camaraderie may be readily perceived, a cheerful familiarity from which neither age nor social rank exclude the duke. In a rondeau to a certain Fredet, Charles refers to a monetary gift that he claims to regret:

> Se regrettez voz dolens jours,
> Et je regrette mon argent
> Que j'ay delivré franchement
> Cuidant de vous donner secours.[4] (2: 349)

> [And if you regret your sorrowful days,
> I regret my money
> That I generously delivered,
> Believing I was giving you help.]

The details associated with the donation (the size of the gift, its purpose, any stipulated conditions, the use or misuse that eventually resulted) as well as other attendant circumstances (similar misappropriations, Fredet's financial reputation, the relationship between the two men, specific incidents to which the passage may subtly allude) all color the audience's reception of the verses. Like so many passages of the *Testament,* the passage draws on extratextual connections perceptible only to the immediate audience.

In another rondeau he playfully ridicules the sexual misadventures of his secretary, Etienne Le Gout, borrowing terms from Latin grammar to heighten the satire:

> Quant rencontré a un acusatif
> Qui sa robe lui a fait ablative;
> De fenestre assez superlative
> A fait un sault portant coups en passif. (2: 301)

> [When he encountered an accusative
> Who made an ablative of his robe;
> From a rather superlative window
> He leaped, taking blows in the passive.]

Again, the humorous intent of the passage presupposes the reader's ability to juxtapose the poetic description with knowledge of the actual episode.

As in the case of the *Testament,* possible distortions in the poet's self-characterizations can only be perceived by measuring the portrait against its subject. In a seemingly morose assessment of his existence he states:

> Le monde est ennuyé de moy,
> Et moy pareillement de lui;
> Je ne congois rien au jour d'ui
> Dont il me chaille que bien poy. (2: 397)

> [The world is tired of me
> And I of it;
> I know nothing these days
> For which I care more than a little.]

Taken as a frank admission of the feelings of boredom and uselessness brought on by old age, the passage is sometimes interpreted as evidence of an increasingly depressed state of mind.[5] Such an interpretation, although possible, disregards the potential for irony. Like Villon, Charles d'Orléans proves quite adept at self-parody, as demonstrated in the following description of the poet taken from one of his later ballades:

> Portant harnoys rouillé de Nonchaloir,
> Sus monture foulee de Foiblesse,
> Mal abillé de Desireus Vouloir . . . (1:168)

> [Wearing armor rusted by Indifference,
> On a steed trampled by Weakness,
> Poorly dressed in Craving Desire.]

What appears, therefore, to be a candid confession may simply be a bit of humorous hyperbole intended for the amusement of an audience capable of distinguishing between the man and the mask.

The poetry of Charles d'Orléans, like that of other late medieval poets, incorporates various details of the actual biographical circumstances surrounding its composition.[6] These circumstances, as I have attempted to demonstrate, cannot be dissociated from the intended audience. But beyond the immediate personal connections between the poet and his audience, there is a larger question—and one much more difficult to address—involving the influence of a literary milieu. To what extent does the poetry of Charles d'Orléans reflect the aesthetic taste of a specific, well-defined audience? Daniel Poirion vaguely attempts at several points in *Le Poète et le prince* to answer the question:

> La création à Blois est détendue, souriante, presque familiale.
>
> [Creation at Blois is relaxed, smiling, almost familial.]
>
> Cette collaboration poétique est beaucoup plus intime que celle d'un concours bourgeois. Elle dépend pour une large part des circonstances de la vie de cour.
>
> [This poetic collaboration is much more intimate than that of a bourgeois competition. It depends in large part on the circumstances of court life.]
>
> Blois où va s'installer Charles d'Orléans restera plutôt un salon qu'un centre d'industrie artistique.[7]
>
> [Blois, where Charles d'Orléans is going to settle, will remain rather a literary salon than a center of artistic industry.]

In a later work Poirion attempts to broadly define the aesthetic criteria of the court of Blois, but he clearly indicates that his definition is tentative and conjectural rather than based on verifiable observations:

> Les contemporains ont-ils apprécié le sourire du prince, à une époque où l'on était plus habitué au burlesque, à la farce, au gras libertinage, ou à la raillerie appuyée? Il semble que cette finesse et cette discrétion, dans le rire comme dans les larmes, définissent le goût du petit cénacle qui a entouré Charles d'Orléans.[8]

[Did the contemporaries appreciate the smile of the prince, at a time when people were more accustomed to burlesque, farce, frank licentiousness, or heavy-handed sarcasm? It seems that this finesse, this discretion, in laughter as well as in tears, define the taste of the little literary circle that surrounded Charles d'Orléans.]

Clearly, the role of milieu in the work of Charles d'Orléans cannot be neglected. Just as the pomp, splendor, and self-importance of the Burgundian court inspired an oratorical and somewhat grandiose strain of poetry, the effect of the festive atmosphere of Blois with its passion for refined amusement can be seen in the verse of the poet-prince and those who wrote under his influence. The problem in attempting to isolate the influence of Blois is that this milieu, with all its Italianate sophistication, elegance, and polished cultivation, was itself the creation of the poet. Thus, while the interaction of Charles d'Orléans with his literary coterie is evident and the possibilities for reciprocal influence are readily apparent, it is virtually impossible to assess the extent to which Charles's poetry reponds to external aesthetic criteria.

Given the difficulty of isolating the influence of Charles d'Orléans's *cénacle,* a group about which we are relatively well informed, the task of defining the role of Villon's literary milieu is one which Villon scholarship, in its present state, is obviously not equipped to carry out. Nonetheless, Villon's little *cénacle* may well have played a significant part in the formation of his poetics. The most basic motive for writing, many would argue, is to please one's readers—to amuse, entertain, instruct, and favorably impress those who receive the work. To achieve this objective, it is essential that the author have at least some vague notion of the kind of reader he hopes to please and a general concept of the aesthetic values of his reader.

If Villon in fact directed much of his poetry to a particular public, then it follows that these portions of his work respond in some degree to the aesthetic taste exhibited by his audience. As in the case of emotional response, the fact that the aesthetics of

Villon's audience cannot be accurately defined does not detract from their potential importance. Stanley Fish has popularized the term "interpretive communities," arguing that a given group of readers may theoretically apply a common reading strategy.[9] It should be remembered that Villon wrote for his own "interpretive community," and his work therefore bears the imprint of the values, attitudes, and aesthetic standards of his public.

conclusion

$\mathbf{a}$ s I observed in my preface, reader-oriented criticism has so far been applied mainly to postmedieval texts. The potential applications of reader-response theory to medieval literature remain largely unexplored. Although it is generally recognized that readerships of different historical periods will approach a literary work from different perspectives, apply different reading strategies, and may ultimately create divergent readings of the same text, little effort has been made to study the ways in which works of literature, especially those of the medieval period, are molded to "fit" the contemporary audience for which they were originally created.[1]

Hans Robert Jauss, the leading proponent of *Rezeptionsästhetik,* introduces a historical element into reader-response criticism with the term "horizon of expectations." Jauss is especially interested in establishing the criteria by which readers of any given period judge a literary work: "The reconstruction of the horizon of expectations, on the basis of which a work in the past was created and received, enables us to find the questions to which the text originally answered and thereby to discover how the reader of that day viewed and understood the work."[2] The concept of the reader's "horizon of expectations" is a useful construct for theoretical purposes, but the utility and feasibility of its application to specific texts remain to be proved. I suggested in Chapter 7 that Villon's poetry undoubtedly reflects the aesthetic taste of his immediate audience. Beyond this general acknowledgement, I do not see how present-day scholarship can define the criteria by which contemporary readers evaluated Villon's poetry. It is also clear from a careful reading of the text that the author makes certain presuppositions concerning his reader. For the purposes of this particular study, I find the author's "horizon of expectations" more enlightening and more amenable to analysis than the reader's expectations of the author.

To return to the thesis outlined in the preface, I believe that the *Testament* read today and the *Testament* read by Villon's first readers are two very different poems. The relationship between the modern reader and the text inevitably produces adversarial encounters. We wrestle with slippery passages and vainly attempt to tie down elusive meanings, constantly on guard against diversionary tactics that could conceal the author's actual intention. It is generally acknowledged that the *Testament* is a "difficult" poem. But when we describe the poem in this way, we are commenting more on our relationship to the poem than on any inherent qualities of the text itself. I do not believe that Villon's first readers found the *Testament* a difficult work—complex, richly layered, somewhat loosely structured, perhaps, but not perplexing or inscrutable. The relationship between the intended reader and the text is based on collaboration and collusion rather than adversarial engagement.

The *Testament* read by Villon's contemporaries was in many ways a more colorful poem than the work we read today. I do not mean to imply that the modern reader will find the *Testament*, where vivid imagery clearly dominates abstract expression, to be a pale poem. But much of the imagery, closely connected to individuals, places, objects irretrievably lost to the past, cannot be actualized by the modern reader. Although the *Testament* is intended to draw on the reader's memory as well as his imagination, we can supply only the latter. Thus, the poem originally had an imaginal quality fundamentally different from that it possesses today.

Humor provides another point of comparison. No reader can miss the humorous intent so frequently manifested in the *Testament*. Villon's humor is richly varied, ranging from the subtlest innuendo to the most blatant satire. But like his imagery, Villon's humor often assumes the reader's familiarity with those who are the target of ridicule. The vague image of a man running through the streets of Paris in dainty slippers, publicly exposing his blemished legs, may be one that the modern reader (once he has identified Villon's victim and has been apprised of the equivocal use of the word *placques*) will find slightly amusing, but it is highly doubtful that the scene will elicit a prolonged burst of laughter. Humor, as a contemporary philosopher observes, normally involves a process of devaluation: "De-valuing, however it is to be analyzed, seems to be neither a precondition of amusement nor the result of it. It is, rather, the amusement itself."[3] It follows that in order to be successfully carried out, devaluation must work against an understanding of the "value" attached to the person or thing subject to ridicule. Without an appreciation of the specific characteristics that Villon devalues in each of his caricatures, the thrust of the humor is weakened. Thus, forceful satire is often reduced to superficial derision. The farcical quality of the *Testament* has been largely lost.

Aside from the adjectives "complex" and "difficult," the terms most frequently applied to the *Testament* in contemporary criticism are "problematic" and "ambiguous." Again, I maintain that both these terms describe the rapport between a modern audience and the poem rather than intrinsic characteristics of the text itself. To conclude that, because we *find* the work problematic, it *is* problematic assumes a natural but logically indefensible inference. The chief cause of our difficulty with Villon's work is a lack of *points de repère,* allowing us to establish a reliable correspondence between the text and the reality it reflects or distorts. The difficulty is most acute in the instances where Villon refers to himself. To assume that all these references are necessarily ironical—a tempting but unacceptably simplistic solution—does not alleviate the difficulty confronting the modern reader. In many cases we may feel reasonably confident that we have correctly understood the intent of a given passage, and indeed, without unconsciously ascribing intentions to the author and attempting to discern changes of tone, the reading of the poem would be a rather uninteresting, mechanical, and even meaningless experience. Still, we must recognize the limitations of our interpretive endeavors. Although we read the poem against our own image of the poet, the work was written for readers who could not help reading the poem against the man himself. I seriously doubt that these readers found the poem problematic in any sense of the word.

Nor is it likely that they were troubled by the ambiguity that has caused modern readers so much perplexity. To describe Villon's work as inherently ambiguous implies either a state of ambivalence or a deceitful intent on the part of the poet. The vast majority of readers and critics, whatever else they might debate, would certainly agree that Villon's poetry is rarely if ever ambivalent; the strongly opinionated quality of his work is evident even to those unable to determine which particular opinion is expressed at a given moment. The most common view is that the *Testament* contains patterns of ambiguity that demonstrate a deceitful purpose. Attributing a fraudulent design to the poem, the reader naturally finds himself in the adversarial stance described earlier.

I would argue that a distinction must be made between deliberate ambiguity with the intent to mislead and equivocal language designed to humorously disguise but not conceal the author's intent. The passage describing the "prayer" that Villon plans to offer for Thibaut d'Aussigny is filled with equivocal phrases, but there is nothing ambiguous about the poet's attitude toward his former captor. The combination of obscure and transparent passages in the *Testament* may be explained either as the result of authorial intent or as the inevitable result of an accelerated "aging process" by which once transparent passages have long ago, at least as early as the time of Marot, been rendered obscure. The second hypothesis, in my opinion, is more plausible, being more consistent with all that may be deduced concerning Villon's rapport with his first readers. If "ambiguous" is defined as "leaving the intended sense doubtful" and if the text is described as it was designed to function with its intended audience rather than as it functions with the readers who have inherited it, then one may justifiably assert, at the risk of blaspheming a cherished doctrine of Villon criticism, that the *Testament* is *not* an ambiguous work.

The basic difference separating Villon's earliest readership from later readerships may be reduced to a single word—sensitivity. From a close study of his poetry, it is clear that Villon expected his audience to discern variations of tone, nuances of meaning, shadings of connotation, subtle gradations of irony. This capacity for discernment is partly related to a common language, not only standard French of fifteenth-century Paris but also a marginal language associated with Villon's milieu, which attached special meanings to certain words and phrases and thus created numerous possibilities for inside jokes. Pierre Demarolle suggests that the comprehension of Villon's poetry requires a knowledge of the *langage équivoque* used by Villon and his peers:

> D'un point de vue pratique, en ce qui concerne la compréhension des textes de Villon à notre époque, il s'agit en fait d'apprendre un second langage, parallèle à la langue commune du temps, de manière à éviter les naïvetés que le critique reproche ironiquement à certains érudits modernes.[4]

> [From a practical point of view, concerning the comprehension of Villon's texts in our own day, it's actually a question of learning a second language, parallel to the common language of his day, in order avoid the naive interpretations for which critics reproach certain modern scholars.]

But the men for whom Villon wrote had more in common with the poet than just a common language, and there is every reason to believe that the *Testament* was written for a warmly receptive audience. The poem, permeated by a spirit of camaraderie, is hardly the private musing of a reclusive mind. On the contrary, at every turn it manifests an awareness of its audience and a playful desire to engage this audience in every possible manner.

Excluded from Villon's "fraternity" of readers, it is inevitable that the modern reader should experience a certain sense of alienation, which is compounded by the "alterity" (Jauss's term) of any medieval text. Putting the *Testament* into a historical perspective and comparing its initial potentialities with those it presently retains, one can hardly escape the conclusion that Villon's poem has lost a substantial amount of its original resiliency. This observation need not lead to a judgmental evaluation—the conclusion, for example, that the *Testament* has in many places been badly eroded by the passage of time and has thus been reduced to an "inferior" condition. The evaluation of relative aesthetic merit is irrelevant to this study. Still, the secure position held by Villon's poetry in the canon of medieval literature should not blind us to the fact that however timeless certain selections may appear, most of his poetry is tightly moored to historical circumstances. Perhaps the most striking paradox of Villon's poetry is the universality achieved by a poet whose work has such a pronounced "local" character.

Whether Villon's relationship with his first readers constitutes an exceptional case in the history of medieval literature, I will leave for others to decide. But I believe that the study of medieval texts with the goal of extrapolating the author's expectations of his reader/listener need not be limited to instances where the relationship between the author and the reader is relatively well defined. It is not difficult to envision potentially productive applications of this critical orientation to numerous works of medieval French literature. What does the text of the *Quinze Joies de mariage* tell us about the author's presuppositions concerning the attitudes of his reader? Or, to push further into the past, what may we learn about the relationship of Marie de France and her immediate audience by studying certain revealing passages of her *Lais?* By shifting attention from the text itself to the rapport between the author and the audience that underlies the text, we may become aware of a new literary vista that still remains vastly unexplored.

notes

Preface

1. Chandler B. Beall, "Dante and His Reader," *Forum Italicum* 13 (1970), 299–343. Marina S. Brownlee, *The Status of the Reading Subject in the Libro de Buen Amor* (Chapel Hill: North Carolina Studies in the Romance Languages and Literatures, 1985). David F. Hult, *Self-Fulfilling Prophecies: Readership and Authority in the First Roman de la Rose* (Cambridge: Cambridge University Press, 1986). Per Nykrog, "Playing Games with Fiction: *Les Quinze Joyes de mariage, Il Corbaccio, El Arcipreste de Talavera*," in *The Craft of Fiction*, ed. Leigh Arrathoon (Rochester, Mich.: Solaris Press, 1984), pp. 423–451.

2. Gert Pinkernell, *François Villons Lais* (Heidelburg: Carl Winter, 1979), p. 14.

Chapter 1

1. Stanley Fish, *Is There a Text in This Class?* (Cambridge: Harvard University Press, 1980), pp. 48–49.

2. Stanley Fish, *Surprised by Sin: The Reader in Paradise Lost* (London and New York: Saint Martin's Press, 1967).

3. Louise Rosenblatt, "On the Aesthetic as the Basic Model of the Reading Process," *Bucknell Review* 28 (1980), 17–32.

4. Wayne C. Booth, *The Rhetoric of Fiction* (Chicago: University of Chicago Press, 1961), pp. 104–105.

5. Jean-Claude Muhlethaler, for example, in his recent *Poétiques du quinzième siècle* (Paris: Nizet, 1983) refers occasionally to the relationship between Villon and his public but refrains from commenting on the nature of the audience itself.

6. Jean Rychner and Albert Henry, ed., *Le Testament Villon* (Geneva: Droz, 1974), 1668–1670. All subsequent citations from the *Testament* are taken from this edition. Citations from other poems by Villon, unless otherwise specified, are taken from Jean Rychner and Albert Henry, eds., *Le Lais Villon et les poèmes variés* (Geneva: Droz, 1977).

7. Hans Robert Jauss, "Literary History as a Challenge to Literary Theory," *New Literary History* 2 (1970–1971), 10.

8. The translation is from Galway Kinnell, *The Poems of François Villon* (Boston: Houghton Mifflin, 1977), p. 135. All English translations of Villon's poetry (unless otherwise indicated) are from Galway Kinnell, *The Poems of François Villon* (Boston: Houghton Mifflin, 1977).

9. Pierre Champion, *François Villon* (Paris: Champion, 1913), p. 65.

10. Gert Pinkernell describes the audience to which the *Lais* is addressed as "un groupe de jeunes voyous cultivés, c'est-à-dire l'entourage du poète des années 1455/56, consistant avant tout en étudiants échoués et en prêtres restés sans prébende" ("a group of young, cultivated hooligans, that is to say the entourage of the poet in the years 1455–1456, consisting above all of unsuccessful students and priests left without a prebend"). See his "François Villon, La Ballade des contrevérités: Aphorismes pour un public criminel," *Zeitschrift für Romanische Philolgie* 101 (1985), 28–44. Except for the dates, Pinkernell's characterization of the first audience of the *Lais* may be applied, with equal validity I believe, to the earliest readers of the *Testament*.

11. Pierre Michel, ed., *François Villon: Poésies complètes* (Paris: Livre de Poche, 1972), p. vi.

12. Louise M. Rosenblatt, *The Reader, the Text, the Poem* (Carbondale: Southern Illinois University Press, 1978), p. 28: "The reader of a text who evokes a literary work of art is, above all, a performer, in the same sense that a pianist performs a sonata, reading it from the text before him."

13. Pierre Champion, ed., *Charles d'Orléans: Poésies*, 2 vols. (Paris: Champion, 1924–1927), 1: 37.

Chapter 2

1. Nigel Wilkins, ed., *Guillaume de Machaut: La Louange des dames* (New York: Harper and Row, 1973), p. 72.

2. Hans Robert Jauss, *Aesthetic Experience and Literary Hermeneutics*, trans. Michael Shaw (Minneapolis: University of Minnesota Press, 1982), p. 264.

3. Allan Paivio, a leading researcher in the field of psychological imagery, admits that numerous questions remain concerning the conceptual relation between poetic imagery and psychological imagery and suggests that a "collaborative effort between poet and psycholinguist might prove to be a mutually profitable approach to such questions." *Imagery and Verbal Processes* (New York: Holt, Rinehart and Winston, 1971), p. 471.

4. Ian Begg, "Imagery and Language," in *Imagery: Current Theory, Research, and Application*, ed. A. A. Sheikh (New York: John Wiley, 1983), p. 305.

5. Ibid., p. 293.

6. David Kuhn, *La Poétique de François Villon* (Paris: Armand Colin, 1967), p. 333.

7. David A. Fein, *A Reading of Villon's Testament* (Birmingham, Ala.: Summa Publications, 1984), p. 76.

8. Louis Thuasne, ed., *François Villon, Oeuvres*, 3 vols. (Paris: Picard, 1923), 2: 122.

9. *Le Testament Villon*, 2: 34.

10. Evelyn B. Vitz, *The Crossroads of Intention: A Study of Symbolic Expression in the Poetry of François Villon* (The Hague: Mouton, 1974), p. 23.

11. Kuhn, *La Poétique*, pp. 123–124.

12. The majority of these hypotheses are summarized by Jean Dufournet in the notes of his latest edition of the *Testament*. *François Villon, Poésies* (Paris: Imprimerie nationale, 1984), pp. 287–288.

13. Thuase, *François Villon*, 3: 524.

14. Norman N. Holland, *5 Readers Reading* (New Haven: Yale University Press, 1975).

15. The same point applies to verse 828: "Par moy, plus maigre que chimere" ("For me, skinnier than a madman"). To what degree does the description distort or correspond to the poet's physical appearance? The true nature of the image can only be appreciated by comparing it to the actual condition of the person it claims to represent.

16. Jean Dufournet in *Nouvelles recherches sur le Testament de François Villon* (Paris: Champion, 1980) interprets the *Abreuvoir Popin* as suggesting "une soif inextinguible" (p. 94); basing his opinion on verses 155–156 of the *Lais*, he describes Raguier as "un gourmet toujours à l'affût du meilleur morceau" (95) ("a gourmet always in quest of the best morsel").

17. Dufournet, *Nouvelles recherches*, p. 97.

18. *Le Testament Villon*, 2: 221: "le fait que tous les légataires de Villon sont des personnages réels, y compris Marion l'Idole et la grande Jehanne de Bretagne, qui suivent la Grosse Margot et lui ressemblent comme deux soeurs, nous incite à croire à la réalité de ce personnage." ("the fact that all of Villon's legatees are actual people, including Marion l'Idole and the big Jehanne de Bretagne, who follow the Grosse Margot and resemble her like two sisters, leads us to believe in the reality of this character").

19. Rosenblatt, *The Reader, the Text, the Poem*, p. 12.

Chapter 3

1. Grace Frank finds little evidence of contrition in this passage and in similar passages of the poem; "The Impenitence of François Villon," *Romanic Review* 37 (1946), 225–236. Janis L. Pallister, in a more convincing demonstration, points to the importance of theology in Villon's poetry; "Attrition and Contrition in the Poetry of François Villon," *Romance Notes* 11 (1969), 392–398.

2. John Fox describes the dilemma of the modern reader trying to discern irony from sincerity in Villon's poetry: "the reader inevitably wonders about its degree of authenticity . . . and ponders on probabilities." *Villon: Poems* (London: Grand and Cutler, 1984), p. 31.

3. Vitz, *The Crossroads of Intention*, p. 20.

4. William Calin, "Observations on Point of View and the Poet's Voice in Villon," *L'Esprit Créateur* 7 (1967), 185.

5. Norris Lacy, "Villon in His Work: the *Testament* and the Problem of Personal Poetry," *L'Esprit Créateur* 18 (1978), 68.

6. Booth, *The Rhetoric of Fiction*, p. 304.

7. Wolfgang Iser, "Interaction Between Text and Reader," in *The Reader and the Text*, eds. Susan Suleiman and Inge Crosman (Princeton: Princeton University Press, 1980), p. 111.

8. Ibid.

9. Wayne C. Booth in *The Rhetoric of Irony* (Chicago: University of Chicago Press, 1974) outlines four steps the reader must perform in order to perceive "stable irony":

1. "The reader is required to reject the literal meaning."

2. "Alternative interpretations or explanations are tried out."

3. "A decision must therefore be made about the author's knowledge or beliefs."

4. "Having made a decision about the knowledge or beliefs of the speaker, we can finally choose a new meaning" (pp. 10–12). The weak link in the modern reader's attempt to identify irony in Villon's work is step 3. Any decision we make regarding the author's beliefs will ultimately be grounded on textual evidence alone. The intended reader obviously possesses a more reliable basis for his decision.

10. Stephen G. Nichols, "François Villon," in *European Writers*, ed. W. T. H. Jackson (New York: Scribners, 1983), 2: 560.

Chapter 4

1. Paul Zumthor, *Essai de poétique médiévale* (Paris: Editions du Seuil, 1972).

2. Walker Gibson, "Authors, Speakers, Readers, and Mock Readers," in *Reader-Response Criticism*, ed. Jane P. Tompkins (Baltimore: Johns Hopkins University Press, 1980), pp. 1–6.

3. Kuhn refers to this hypothetical reader as the *lecteur moyen*, whom he finds only of incidental interest; he concentrates on other facets of the passage. *La Poétique*, p. 240.

4. Kinnell, *The Poems of François Villon*, p. 27.

5. Muhlethaler, *Poétiques du quinzième siècle*, p. 57.

6. Odette Petit-Morphy, *François Villon et la scholastique*, 2 vols. (Paris: Champion, 1977), 1: 444.

7. Rychner, *Lais*, verses 67, 275.

8. I have elsewhere discussed at greater length the tension between the temporal dimensions of the *Testament* and the philosophical implications of this opposition. See "Time and Timelessness in Villon's *Testament*," *Neophilologus* 71 (1987), 470–473.

9. Acrostic signatures are also found in three ballades outside the *Testa-*

ment: the "Ballade des contre-vérités," the "Débat du coeur et du corps," and the "Ballade de bon conseil."

10. Jonathan Culler, *The Pursuit of Signs: Semiotics, Literature, Deconstruction* (Ithaca: Cornell University Press, 1981), p. 50.

11. Karl D. Uitti, "A Note on Villon's Poetics," *Romance Philology* 30 (1976), 187–192.

12. Kuhn, *La Poétique*, p. 60.

13. Edelgard DuBruck, "Villon's Two Pleas for Absolution," *L'Esprit Créateur* 7 (1967), 192.

14. David A. Fein, "An Unexplored Acrostic in Villon's *Testament*," *Fifteenth-Century Studies* 6 (1983), 115–119.

Chapter 5

1. For a description of the satirical testament in its Latin, French, and non-French vernacular form, see Winthrop H. Rice, *The European Ancestry of Villon's Satirical Testaments* (New York: Corporate Press, 1941). To appreciate the extent to which Villon draws on the legal and religious language employed in actual fifteenth-century wills, one only has to compare the *Testament* to a few of the documents contained in Alexandre Tuetey's *Testaments enregitrés au Parlement de Paris sous le règne de Charles VI* (Paris: Imprimerie Nationale, 1880).

2. Philippe Ariès in *L'Homme devant la mort* (Paris: Editions du Seuil, 1977) summarizes the religious function of the late medieval will: "Donc, à la fin de sa vie, le fidèle confesse sa foi, reconnaît ses péchés et les rachète par un acte public, écrit *ad pias causas*" (188) ("Then, at the end of his life, the religiously faithful man confesses his faith, acknowledges his sins and redeems them by a public act, written *ad pias causas*").

3. Jean Englemann, *Les testaments coutumiers au xvᵉ siècle* (Paris: Macon, 1903), p. 80.

4. For a collection of striking examples of this artistic motif, see Alberto Tenenti, *La vie et la mort à travers l'art du xvᵉ siècle* (Paris: Armand Colin, 1952).

5. Ariès, *L'Homme devant la mort*, p. 190.

6. Jean Dufournet, ed., *François Villon: Poésies* (1984), p. 231. French translation also from this source.

7. André Mary, ed., *Oeuvres de François Villon* (Paris: Garnier, 1970), p. 193.

8. Dufournet, *Poésies* (1984), p. 282.

9. Georges Brunet, *Le Pari de Pascal* (Paris: Brouwer, 1956), p. 134.

10. Chandler Beall in "Dante and His Reader," *Forum Italicum* 13 (1979), 299–343, finds the same didactic element in Dante's relationship with his reader: "Since the principal aim of the poet is the instruction, betterment, and ultimate salvation of his reader, it is natural that the poem should contain occasional admonishments addressed directly to him . . . 'Se Dio ti lasci, lettor, prender frutto / di tua lezione, or pensa per te stesso.'" (p. 317)

11. Pierre-Yves Badel, *Introduction à la vie littéraire du Moyen Age* (Paris: Bordas, 1969), p. 168.

12. Gert Pinkernell, "François Villon, La Ballade des contre-vérités," 30.

13. Vladimir R. Rossman, *Perspectives of Irony in Medieval French Literature* (The Hague: Mouton, 1975), pp. 44–45.

Chapter 6

1. The exceptions are: "Ballade et oroison," "Ballade de la Grosse Margot," "Ballade de mercy" in the *Testament,* and "Epître à ses amis" and "Questions au clerc du guichet." Also, a few poems are addressed to special audiences that are not covered either by the category of "privileged reader" or "anonymous reader": "Louange à Marie d'Orléans," "Louange à la cour," "Requête à Monseigneur de Bourbon."

2. Luke: 6, 37.

3. Italo Siciliano, *François Villon et les thèmes poétiques du moyen âge* (Paris: Armand Colin, 1934), p. 452. Pierre LeGentil, *Villon* (Paris: Hatier, 1967), p. 66.

4. LeGentil, *Villon.* Jean Dufournet uses the same phrase in his introductory comments on the *Testament* in *François Villon: Poésies* (1984), p. 17. Dufournet speculates that Villon omitted "les ballades sur des procédés qu'il jugeait trop faciles . . . ou les pièces alourdies d'allusions mythologiques . . . ou emphatiques" ("the ballades based on techniques that he considered too easy . . . or the bombastic pieces . . . or those loaded with mythical allusions").

5. David Fein, "Joined Hearts and Severed Tongues: An Illustration of Antithetical Juxtaposition in Villon's *Testament.*" *Philological Quarterly* 66 (1987), 315–324.

6. *Le Testament Villon,* 657–664, 673–728, 910–933.

Chapter 7

1. Champion, ed. *Charles d'Orléans: Poésies,* 1: 55–56. All quotations from Charles d'Orléans's poetry are taken from this edition.

2. Walter Slatoff, *With Respect to Readers* (Ithaca: Cornell University Press, 1970), p. 37.

3. Enid McLeod, *Charles d'Orléans: Prince and Poet* (London: Chatto and Windus, 1969) describes the young men who made up the poetic court of Blois: "Each of them was attached to one or the other of the different departments of the household that looked after the provisioning of it in bread, wine, meat and so on, and their duties were the serving of the ducal family and their guests at meals, in the role of carver, cup-bearer and so on. Humble though these tasks sound, the young esquires who performed them were nearly always sons of good and sometimes noble families, who started as pages and occasionally rose in later life to the holding of high offices, not only under their original master but in the State" (p. 299).

4. About Fredet, as in the case of many other contributors to Charles

d'Orléans's album, we know practically nothing, Charles first made his acquaintance in Tours in 1444. His name appears frequently in the album, where he left a *complainte* and several rondeaux.

5. For example, McLeod, *Charles d'Orléans,* 320.

6. As an example of this phenomenon, see Ann Tukey Harrison, "Charles d'Orléans—the Reluctant Traveler," *Fifteenth-Century Studies* 10 (1984), 79–90, a study of the various ways in which the poet's actual travel experiences are reflected in his poetry.

7. Daniel Poirion, *Le Poète et le prince* (Paris: Presses Universitaires de France, 1965), 182, 186, 50.

8. Daniel Poirion, *Le Moyen Age* vol. II (Paris: Artaud, 1971), 218.

9. Fish, *Is There a Text in This Class?*

Conclusion

1. Hans Ulrich Gumbrecht in "Strangeness as a Requirement for Topicality: Medieval Literature and Reception Theory" (*L'Esprit Créateur* 21 (1981), 5–12) suggests that this aspect of medieval literature warrants further investigation: "This general reformulation of issues can be realized through reconstruction of those original communication situations of which the mutual expectations of the text's author and his first readers are the essential constitutents" (p. 7).

2. Jauss,"Literary History as a Challenge to Literary Theory," 18.

3. Roger Scruton, "Laughter," in *The Philosophy of Laughter and Humor,* ed. John Moreall (Albany: State University of New York Press, 1987), p. 168.

4. Pierre Demarolle, *Villon: un testament ambigu* (Paris: Larousse, 1973), p. 105.

BIBLIOGRAPHY

General Criticism

Aries, Philipp. *L'Homme devant la mort*. Paris: Seuil, 1977.

Badel, Pierre-Yves. *Introduction à la vie littéraire du moyen âge*. Paris: Bordas, 1969.

Beall, Chandler B. "Dante and His Reader." *Forum Italicum* 13 (1970), 299–343.

Bleich, David. *Subjective Criticism*. Baltimore: Johns Hopkins University Press, 1978.

Booth, Wayne C. *The Rhetoric of Fiction*. Chicago: University of Chicago Press, 1961.

———. *The Rhetoric of Irony*. Chicago: University of Chicago Press, 1974.

Brownlee, Marina S. *The Status of the Reading Subject in the Libro de Buen Amor*. Chapel Hill: North Carolina Studies in the Romance Languages and Literatures, 1985.

Brunet, Georges. *Le Pari de Pascal*. Paris: Brouwer, 1956.

Champion, Pierre, ed. *Charles d'Orléans: Poésies*. 2 vols. Paris: Champion, 1924–27.

Culler, Jonathan. *The Pursuit of Signs: Semiotics, Literature, Deconstruction*. Ithaca: Cornell University Press, 1981.

Eco, Umberto. *The Role of the Reader: Explorations in the Semiotics of Texts*. Bloomington: Indiana University Press, 1980.

Englemann, Jean. *Les testaments coutumiers au xve siècle*. Paris: Macon, 1903.

Fish, Stanley. *Is There a Text in This Class? The Authority of Interpretive Communities*. Cambridge: Harvard University Press, 1980.

———. *Surprised by Sin: The Reader in Paradise Lost*. New York: Saint Martin's Press, 1967.

Gumbrecht, Hans Ulrich. "Strangeness as a Requirement for Topicality: Medieval Literature and Reception Theory." *L'Esprit Créateur* 21 (1981), 5–12.

Harrison, Ann. "Charles d'Orléans—the Reluctant Traveler." *Fifteenth-Century Studies* 10 (1984), 79–90.

Holub, Robert C. *Reception Theory: A Critical Introduction*. London: Methuen, 1984.

Hult, David F. *Self-Fulfilling Prophecies: Readership and Authority in the First Roman de la Rose.* Cambridge: Cambridge University Press, 1986.

Holland, Norman N. *The Dynamics of Literary Response.* New York: Oxford University Press, 1968.

———. *5 Readers Reading.* New Haven: Yale University Press, 1975.

Iser, Wolfgang. *The Act of Reading: A Theory of Aesthetic Response.* Baltimore: Johns Hopkins University Press, 1978.

———. *The Implied Reader: Patterns of Communication from Bunyan to Beckett.* Baltimore: Johns Hopkins University Press, 1974.

Jauss, Hans Robert. *Aesthetic Experience and Literary Hermeneutics.* Translated by Michael Shaw. Minneapolis: University of Minnesota Press, 1982.

———. "The Alterity and Modernity of Medieval Literature." *New Literary History* 10 (1979), 181–229.

———. "Literary History as a Challenge to Literary Theory." *New Literary History* 2 (1970–1971), 7–37.

———. *Toward an Aesthetic of Reception.* Translated by Timothy Bahti. Minneapolis: University of Minnesota Press, 1982.

Langman, F. H. "The Idea of the Reader in Literary Criticism." *British Journal of Aesthetics* 7 (1967), 84–94.

Mailloux, Stephen. "Reader-Response Criticism?" *Genre* 10 (1977), 413–431.

Mary, André, ed. *Oeuvres de François Villon.* Paris: Garnier, 1970.

McLeod, Enid. *Charles d'Orléans: Prince and Poet.* London: Chatto and Windus, 1969.

Moreall, John, ed. *The Philosophy of Laughter and Humor.* Albany: State University of New York Press, 1987.

Nykrog, Per. "Playing Games with Fiction: *Les Quinze Joyes de mariage, Il Corbaccio, El Arcipreste de Talavera.*" In Leigh Arrathoon, ed., *The Craft of Fiction.* Rochester, Mich.: Solaris Press, 1984. 423–451.

Ong, Walter J., S. J. "The Writer's Audience is Always a Fiction." *Publications of the Modern Language Association* 90 (1975), 9–21.

Paivio, Allan. *Imagery and Verbal Processes.* New York: Holt, Rinehart and Winston, 1971.

Poirion, Daniel. *Le Moyen Age,* vol. 2. Paris: Artaud, 1971.

———. *Le Poète et le prince.* Paris: P. U. F., 1965.

Rabinowitz, Peter. "Truth in Fiction: A Reexamination of Audiences." *Critical Inquiry* 4 (1977), 121–141.

Reichart, John. *Making Sense of Literature.* Chicago: University of Chicago Press, 1977.

Riffaterre, Michael. *Semiotics of Poetry.* Bloomington: Indiana University Press, 1978.

Rosenblatt, Louise. "On the Aesthetic as the Basic Model of the Reading Process." *Bucknell Review* 28 (1980).

———. *The Reader, the Text, the Poem: The Transactional Theory of the Literary Work.* Carbondale: Southern Illinois University Press, 1978.

Rossman, Vladimir. *Perspectives of Irony in Medieval French Literature.* The Hague: Mouton, 1975.

Bibliography

Sheikh, A., ed. *Imagery: Current Theory, Research, and Application.* New York: John Wiley, 1983.

Slatoff, Walter. *With Respect to Readers: Dimenisons of Literary Response.* Ithaca: Cornell University Press, 1970.

Suleiman, Susan, and Inge Crosman, eds. *The Reader in the Text: Essays on Audience and Interpretation.* Princeton: Princeton University Press, 1980.

Teneti, Alberto. *La Vie et la mort à travers l'art du XVe siècle.* Paris: A. Colin, 1952.

Tompkins, Jane, ed. *Reader-Response Criticism: From Formalism to Post-Structuralism.* Baltimore: Johns Hopkins University Press, 1980.

Tuetey, Alexandre. *Testaments enregistrés au Parlement de Paris sous le règne de Charles VI.* Paris: Imprimerie Nationale, 1880.

Wilkins, Nigel, ed. *Guillaume de Machaut: La Louange des dames.* New York: Harper and Row, 1973.

Zumthor, Paul. *Essai de poétique médiévale.* Paris: Seuil, 1972.

Villon

Blakeslee, Merritt R. "Le *Lais* et le *Testament* de François Villon: Essai de lecture freudienne." *Fifteenth-Century Studies* 5 (1982), 1–8.

Burger, André. *Lexique de la langue de Villon.* Geneva: Droz, 1957.

Calin, William. "Observations on Point of View and the Poet's Voice in Villon." *L'Esprit Créateur* 7 (1967), 180–187.

Champion, Pierre. *François Villon.* 2 vols. Paris: Champion, 1913.

Deroy, Jean. *François Villon: recherches sur le Testament.* The Hague: Mouton, 1967.

Demarolle, Pierre. *L'Esprit de Villon.* Paris: Nizet, 1968.

———. "Pour l'interprétation du texte de Villon." *Romance Notes* 14 (1973), 613–620.

———. *Villon: un testament ambigu.* Paris: Larousse, 1973.

Di Stefano, Giuseppe. "Villoniana." *Le Moyen Français* 1 (1977), 149–160.

Dragonetti, Roger. "Le contredit de François Villon." *Modern Language Notes* 98 (1983), 594–623.

DuBruck, Edelgard. "Villon's Two Pleas for Absolution." *L'Esprit Créateur* 7 (1967), 188–196.

Dufournet, Jean. "Les Formes de l'ambiguité dans le *Testament* de Villon." *Revue des Langues Romanes* 86 (1982), 191–219.

———. *François Villon: Poésies.* Paris: Imprimerie Nationale, 1984.

———. *Nouvelles recherches sur le Testament de François Villon.* Paris: Champion, 1980.

———. *Recherches sur le Testament de François Villon.* 2 vols. (2 ed). Paris: Société d'Edition d'Enseignement Supérieur, 1971.

Favier, Jean. *François Villon.* Paris: Fayard, 1982.

Fein, David A. "Joined Hearts and Severed Tongues: An Illustration of Antithetical Juxtaposition in Villon's *Testament*." *Philological Quarterly* 66 (1987), 315–324.

———. *A Reading of Villon's Testament.* Birmingham, Ala.: Summa Publications, 1984.

———. "Time and Timelessness in Villon's *Testament.*" *Neophilologus* 71 (1987), 470–473.

"An Unexplored Acrostic in Villon's *Testament.*" *Fifteenth-Century Studies* 6 (1983), 115–119.

Fox, John. *The Poetry of Villon.* London: Thomas Nelson and Sons, 1962.

———. *Villon: Poems.* London: Grant and Cutler, 1984.

Frank, Grace. "The Impenitence of François Villon." *Romanic Review* 37 (1946), 225–236.

———. "Villon's Poetry and the Biographical Approach." *L'Esprit Créateur* 7 (1967), 159–169.

Guiraud, Pierre. *Le Testament de Villon: ou le gai savoir de la basoche.* Paris: Gallimard, 1970.

Habeck, Fritz. *Villon; ou la légende d'un rebelle.* Translated by Elisabeth Gaspard. Paris: Mercure de France, 1970.

Harrison, Ann Tukey. "The Theme of Authority in the Works of François Villon." *The Centennial Review* 24, 65–78.

Hayes, Joseph J. "Gothic Love and Death: François Villon and the City of Paris." *Journal of Popular Culture* 11 (1978), 719–729.

Imbs, Paul. "Villon scholastique?" *Travaux de Linguistique et de Littérature* 19 (1981), 69–143.

Kinnell, Galway. *The Poems of François Villon.* Boston: Houghton Mifflin, 1977.

Kuhn, David. *La Poétique de François Villon.* Paris: Armand Colin, 1967.

Lacy, Norris. "The Flight of Time: Villon's Trilogy of Ballades." *Romance Notes* 22 (1982), 353–358.

———. "Villon in His Work: the *Testament* and the Problem of Personal Poetry." *L'Esprit Créateur* 18 (1978), 60–69.

LeGentil, Pierre. *Villon.* Paris: Hatier, 1967.

Michel, Pierre, ed. *François Villon: Poésies complètes.* Paris: Livre de Poche, 1972.

Muhlethaler, Jean-Claude. *Poétiques du quinzième siècle: situation de François Villon et Michault Taillevent.* Paris: Nizet, 1983.

Nichols, Stephen G. "François Villon." In *European Writers,* edited by W. T. H. Jackson. New York: Scribners, 1983. 2: 535–570.

Pallister, Janis L. "Attrition and Contrition in the Poetry of François Villon." *Romance Notes* 11 (1969), 392–398.

Payen, Jean-Charles. "Le coup de l'étrier: Villon martyr et Golliard ou comment se faire oublier quand on est immortel?" *Etudes Françaises* 16 (1980), 21–34.

Peckham, Robert D. "François Villon's *Testament* and the Poetics of Transformation." *Fifteenth-Century Studies* 11 (1985), 71–83.

Petit-Morphy, Odette. *François Villon et la scholastique.* 2 vols. Paris: Champion, 1977.

Pickens, Rupert T. "The Concept of the Feminine Ideal in Villon's *Testament:* Huitain LXXXIX." *Studies in Philology* 70 (1973), 42–50.

Pinkernell, Gert. "François Villon, La Ballade des contrevérités: Aphorismes pour un public criminel." *Zeitschrift für Romanische Philologie* 101 (1985), 28–44.

———. *François Villons Lais*. Heidelburg: Carol Winter, 1979.

Regalado, Nancy F. "La Fonction poétique des noms propres dans le *Testament* de François Villon." *Cahiers de l'Association Internationale des Etudes Françises* 32, 51–68.

Rice, Winthrop. *The European Ancestry of Villon's Satirical Testaments*. New York: Corporate Press, 1941.

Rossman, Vladimir R. *François Villon: les concepts médiévaux du testament*. Paris: Jean-Pierre Delarge, 1976.

Rychner, Jean, and Henry Albert, eds. *Le Lais Villon et les poèmes variés*. 2 vols. Geneva: Droz, 1977.

———. *Le Testament Villon*. 2 vols. Geneva: Droz, 1974.

Sargent-Baur, Barbara N. "Personnages bibliques, personnages villoniens." *Etudes de philologie romane . . . offerts à Jules Horrent*, edited by J. d'Heur and N. Cherubini. Liège: s.n., 1980. 391–396.

Siciliano, Italo. *François Villon et les thèmes poétiques du moyen âge*. Paris: Armand Colin, 1934.

Speer, Mary B. "The Editorial Tradition of Villon's *Testament*." *Romance Philology* 31 (1977), 344–361.

Storme, Julie A. "Love in the *Testament*." *Romance Notes* 24 (1984), 270–276.

Terdiman, Richard. "The Structure of Villon's *Testament*." *Publications of the Modern Language Association* 82 (1967), 622–633.

Thuasne, Louis, ed. *François Villon, Oeuvres*. 3 vols. Paris: Picard, 1923.

Uitti, Karl D. "A Note on Villon's Poetics." *Romance Philology* 30 (1976), 187–192.

Vertone, Teodosio. *Rythme, dualité et création poétique dans l'oeuvre de François Villon*. Rome: Lucarini, 1983.

Vitz, Evelyn B. *The Crossroads of Intentions: A Study of Symbolic Expression in the Poetry of François Villon*. The Hague: Mouton, 1974.

Weinmann, Heinz. "L'économie du *Testament* de François Villon." *Etudes Françaises* 16 (1980), 35–61.

Wilkins, Nigel. "François Villon, poète universel." *Romania* 103 (1982), 338–344.

index